LITTLE APPLES
WILL GROW AGAIN

LITTLE APPLES WILL GROW AGAIN

FRED BROWN

ISIS
LARGE PRINT
Oxford

942.084

Copyright © Fred Brown, 2008

First published in Great Britain 2008
by ISIS Publishing Ltd

Published in Large Print 2008 by ISIS Publishing Ltd.,
7 Centremead, Osney Mead, Oxford OX2 0ES
by arrangement with
the Author

British Library Cataloguing in Publication Data
Brown, Fred
    Little apples will grow again. – Large print ed.
    (Isis reminiscence series)
    1. Brown, Fred – Childhood and youth
    2. World War, 1939–1945 – Great Britain
    3. Large type books
    4. Great Britain – Social life and customs –
    1918–1945
    I. Title
    941'.084'092

ISBN 978–0–7531–9462–1 (hb)
ISBN 978–0–7531–9463–8 (pb)

Printed and bound in Great Britain by
T. J. International Ltd., Padstow, Cornwall

Dedication

This book is dedicated to the memory of Mary and Sid who, in troubled times and in a troubled place, raised their large family and raised it well.

CHAPTER ONE

At the Hall

Mary awoke early after a short sleep lying on the stiff, horse-hair mattress on the iron frame bed. She looked about her tiny room and felt happy. She was in the servants' quarters of Capesthorne Hall, the home of the Bromley-Davenport family, near Macclesfield.

The small room was crowded, with a wardrobe, chest of drawers and a chair, all placed far enough from the open fireplace to avoid scorching when the fire was lit. Her picture of the Irish hero Michael Collins was kept hidden in the wardrobe. This was her day off and she dreamily dwelt on the progress she had made during her time at the Hall.

She had left her troubled, war-torn country in 1919 when she was sixteen, and worked hard cleaning the grates, setting the fires, polishing brass, silver and copper, dusting, washing up and preparing vegetables. The cook had noticed this small, hardworking, industrious and intelligent Irish girl and wanted her for the kitchen team, and so she became "apprenticed" to the Fat Cook.

That was five years ago, in 1923. She had learned fast and was now assistant to the Fat Cook. The Fat

Cook knew she was taking a chance with the dark-haired, brown-eyed colleen from the Emerald Isle, and that the girl had witnessed the oppression, violence and bloodshed that had occurred in Ireland leading up to the Home Rule agreement of 1922. She understood why this pretty, young girl would have cause to hate the English.

If Mary did hate the English, she never let it show while she was at the Hall; she was too intelligent for that. She needed the job and the room with the hard bed. She did admire the British aristocracy. She liked their lifestyle, their clothing, their manners and way of speaking. She tried hard to modify her brogue, the rough way in which she spoke, for it was necessary for her to be understood in the busy, work-day atmosphere at the Hall.

She never did master the combined "th" and would "tink" instead of think, and had a "tort" instead of a thought. She did, however, grasp the affectation that the well-spoken gentry applied to some words containing the double "F" sounds. So, "Off" became "awf" and "cough" became "cawf". She did not admire but was amused by the moral hypocrisy of the gentry. She knew, as all the staff did, of the "goings-on" at the frequent weekend parties at the Hall. But the servants would say nothing.

She liked the Fat Cook and the Fat Cook liked her. She had groomed Mary to be her second-in-command. This was another reason for contentment. Yesterday, when the Fat Cook had taken a day off, Mary had taken charge of all the meals for the Master and

2

Mistress and their guests. It hadn't been a big, important occasion — not like when Royalty came to stay, the Fat Cook would have to be in charge then — but it was important enough. In spite of her anxiety, she had coped.

Mary thought of her family on the small two-acre farm in Ireland. They were not really her family, but she wanted them to be. Uncle John and Aunt Rose had raised her from the age of ten, and she had become their little servant, learning to fetch and carry, scrub and clean, muck out the animals, and cut and stack the turf for the fire. Hard work for a small child, but quite normal on small family farms.

Her mother, Bridget, had placed her with Rose's family, the Donnellys, as a "nurse child", which probably meant she was illegitimate. Rose was nine years older than Mary, and when she married John Doyle, Mary joined them on their small farm. The work was hard, but Mary was happy.

Mary's mother returned to England, to the London home of the Bromley-Davenports. Mary never really knew her mother and her feelings towards her were quite neutral, as though she were a distant Aunt. A letter and gift would arrive occasionally, telling of people, places and things which were far-removed from the small farm.

Mary was happy enough with Rose and John, the cow, the goat and the chickens. When Bridget did visit, once or twice in ten years, she seemed quiet, dull and serious, always dressed in black. Mary never did get to know her, but when she was about sixteen, she showed

3

an interest in the people, places and things her mother had written of, and a position was arranged for her at Capesthorne Hall.

Sometimes, if two or three friends who worked at the Hall had days off together, they would catch the bus or train to Manchester and wander down the streets looking into the shop windows, dreaming of owning the beautiful things they saw there. They might also take a charabanc ride into the Peak District to the famous Cat and Fiddle pub and, if a photographer was about, pose for a record of the occasion.

Much as Mary enjoyed those rare trips together with her friends, she also enjoyed lazing the day away in her room, pottering, preening and reading. She loved to read the articles and gossip in the ladies' fashion magazines. These magazines were picked up by staff members after having been read by the Mistress of the house, and passed around for all to read in the servants' quarters. However, it was not wise to have the butler or housekeeper catch you in possession of a magazine.

Mary borrowed books from the local library and read avidly. Her favourites were detective stories, true crimes or stories about the British landed gentry. She was part of this world and although the Masters were English, she loved it, particularly if the tales were humorous. She loved to have the upper classes ridiculed in stories about their rituals, eccentricities, extravagancies, hypocrisy and arrogance.

As a feisty Irish girl who had witnessed the troubles in her homeland and was deeply affected by them, her loyalties were firmly entrenched. On St Patrick's Day, she was proud to wear the largest bunch of shamrock Uncle John could be persuaded to send her, this practice always out of sight of the Master, butler and housekeeper. The Fat Cook understood, though.

CHAPTER TWO

A New Recruit

This day she would make sure she visited the kitchen for her lunch. She had missed breakfast. As it had to be taken so early, it would not have allowed her the luxury of a lie-in. A small break in routine would occur today, as the butler was to receive a new member of staff: a footman. This man would need to be briefed by the butler about his duties as door attendant, and about table service and waiting, as well being given the costly and flamboyant livery he'd be expected to wear.

What sort of a man, thought Mary, would want to be dressed like a peacock, waiting at the table, opening doors, bending to the whims of the Masters and bullied by a pompous butler? They are usually ex-Army, she mused, maybe some of the very devils who tried to break the Irish spirit. They didn't usually last long in the job, particularly if they were in France in the Great War. They wouldn't take orders from some puff-chested old boy in pinstriped trousers, after what they had been through.

The staff had to eat in shifts, so the lunch period would last two hours. Mary left her room in the attic of the great, rambling, Victorian mansion to cover the whole two hours. Being a favourite of the fat cook, Mary was allowed to linger in the kitchen as long as she liked on her days off. This was where all the servants ate, and the Fat Cook, a quiet person herself, loved Mary's constant chatter. She was amused by her stories of her homeland and colourful phrases in soft Irish brogue. This was the Fat Cook's territory; even the puffy butler had no power here. Mary could be herself. Her chatter was brought to an abrupt end when the butler entered with his new charge, and introduced him as Sydney Brown.

At the age of 25, Mary often wondered whether she would ever marry and have children. For this reason, together with all the other eligible maidens on the staff, they would look with interest at any new male joining the household, fine livery wearers or otherwise.

One of her staff friends, Michael, thought of Mary as his girl and Mary was willing to refer to Michael as her boyfriend. The relationship was without passion and so Mary was still a virgin. She would need to be certain of the man she gave herself to, as her strict Catholic upbringing, the firm guidance of Uncle John and Aunt Rose and the secrecy surrounding her own parenting, endowed her with a strong moral conscience. Anyway, she enjoyed her life as it was, she liked her job with the fat cook, her books and magazines and her tiny room with the hard bed.

She eyed Sydney Brown. He was about her age, light of build and thin, a little taller than herself, making him about 5'8". His hair was mid-brown and wispy; a small wave would often flop forward on his forehead. His skin was tanned and swarthy, his hooked nose made him look like an Arab or a Jew, but his piercing blue eyes placed him firmly within a Northern European race.

Mary was interested. He was not dashingly handsome, but the combination of features, she observed, told her there was more to this man than the average servant. He was smartly dressed in a mid-grey suit, his shoes were highly polished; everything about him said "ex-Army". Thank God they didn't present him in the peacock's clothes, which Mary thought would have robbed him of his dignity.

The butler was relentless with his instructions to his new recruit, and carried on the briefing during lunch in order to quickly stamp his authority and control on the newcomer. This was much to the annoyance of all the eligible young ladies at the table, who were waiting to know more of this presentable young man.

Mary closely observed Sydney's reactions to the verbal barrage from the butler, and saw it all in his blue eyes. They did not look fearful or angry; they looked quietly confident, knowing and cheeky, as if telling that this puffed-up windbag would be dealt with in the course of time. The newcomer was playing a patient waiting game. She admired such a spirited man and once, during his lecture, when the butler turned to a staff member to confirm a point, Sydney stole the moment to cast a knowing wink at Mary. Cheeky young man, she thought, but she was excited just the same.

Sydney seemed to be controlling the pace and ferocity of the briefing by simple timed movements and gestures. He'd drop something, request the condiments, cough or scratch. Rather than openly annoying the butler, it left him with a puzzled look, which said, "Is this man an idiot or just pulling my leg?" Of course, he would never think that Sydney was just being devilishly manipulative. Mary understood; this was the game the Irish had been playing on the English for centuries.

The game that had put the butler out of his stride was quietly admired and applauded by all persons at the table. They had all, at some point, had a tongue lashing from the butler. They also knew that this newcomer would not remain long at the Hall.

Mary spent the remainder of her day wondering and thinking while walking in the estate parkland where staff were allowed. She could not get this mischievous, subtle man out of her mind. She thought he must have Irish blood in him. She wouldn't have much time to get to know him, only seeing him at mealtimes and even then with a table full of staff. Mary wondered if that glanced wink across the table was a sign that he could care for her. She looked forward to their next meeting, the following day, when she would be cooking and serving the staff lunches.

Taking care, as she always did with her cooking, she anxiously watched the entrance to the kitchen that led from the Master's quarters, for that was where Sydney would arrive for lunch. She was not looking forward to seeing him in the 18th century dandy's clothes he would be wearing. Those shiny, patent, large buckled shoes, the white stockings fitted to just below the knee, the puffed, bright coloured breeches and the frilly, cuffed and cravatted coat. Thank heavens they no longer make them wear the powdered wigs that the court lawyers wear, she thought.

She need not have worried, for the opening of the door was as a stage curtain rising for Sydney. He minced in on his toes as delicately as a ballet dancer, short-pacing, his arms held out at shoulder height, limp-wristed. Holding this pose, he strutted towards Mary, who was ladling out the stew at the stove. He pointed his right foot before his left, and with an exaggerated flutter of the handkerchief, took a bow, saying, "Lady Mary, your servant awaits".

Mary dropped the ladle back into the stew and felt her face flush with embarrassment. The assembled staff let out a very loud roar of laughter, which brought the butler hurrying and puffing into the kitchen. Angrily, he quickly suppressed the mirth and rebuked the company, but by this time Sydney was innocently sitting at the table, quietly enjoying his stew. Shocked, and her heart beating wildly, Mary took a while to regain her composure and continued nervously to carry out her duties. She was not too shocked to notice the innocent act of the young man in the foppish clothes, though. The lights were out, the theatre closed, the butler had missed the performance, he never knew who the leading man was.

The scene had caused much excitement among the more lowly members of staff, and much later Mary heard stories of Sydney's antics in other parts of the house where she was no longer required to visit. Sydney

10

would take any opportunity to slide down the banister in his full livery, hooting loudly and legs wide astride. He also repeated his bowing act when he needed to pass wind, and the combination of dandy, bowing and farting greatly amused the housemaids present, busy scrubbing, polishing and cleaning. Many times they would wet themselves trying to suppress the giggles.

Mary trusted that he would not repeat that routine in the kitchen, but admired the tactic and enjoyed the light-heartedness it brought to otherwise dull routines. With large echoing halls and corridors, it was only a matter of time before the sounds of frivolity reached the ears of authority.

Sydney joined Mary's little group of friends on their trips out when they had days off together. Michael soon became aware of Mary's interest in Sydney and knew he was not her number one boyfriend anymore. He never liked Sydney, never understood the subtlety of some of his antics and was amazed by the cheekiness and recklessness of his actions. He wanted to keep his job, he worked hard and toed the line as a groom; he listened and obeyed. He tolerated Sydney tagging along with the group, but suffered when he saw Mary and Sydney were falling in love.

It wasn't long before the outings became just for two. Mary and Sydney would take long country walks together, talking and laughing and trying to sort out the problems of the world. On Irish matters, a compromise was reached. Sydney had decided there was no dealing with the irrational, sentimental, passionate and unforgiving nature of the Irish. The matter was insoluble, but Mary remained entrenched with that nature and, far from spoiling their relationship, it enhanced it. Sydney was a master of making fun of such attitudes and his wit, more often than not, would have to save him from a punch, a thrown saucepan or whatever was to hand from the angered. Sydney's talk would range from the ridiculous, which Mary loved, to the sublime, which she often failed to understand, but listened bewildered to his ramblings nonetheless.

She was not surprised, therefore, when after a few months of meeting, courting and walking, he one day started off in his "sublime" mood. However, it did surprise her that after several hours together, she still hadn't seen the ridiculous side of his nature. This worried her. Had he suddenly lost interest in her? Was he ill?

His condition remained for days; he talked less, ate less and no longer joked. His eyes were watery, with an occasional running tear, and his shoulders sagged. Mary needed to know what was wrong and managed to confront him.

"Oh, it's nothing", he said. "I'll be all right in a day or two." His voice was unconvincing and Mary suspected he suffered from the nervous complaint many veterans of the Great War had. She'd seen many of them pass though the Hall, not being able to hold down a job for more than a few months.

But Sydney had told her he hadn't been in France during the war, and hadn't experienced the worst battles. Although only a boy of seventeen, the Army had sent him to India where rebellious tribes were taking advantage while most of the British and Indian troops were otherwise occupied in Europe.

When she next had the opportunity to quiz him, she asked again about his condition.

"Oh, I was like this before I went in the Army", he said.

It was too late. By this time Mary was deeply in love, and when Mary loved, she loved forever.

CHAPTER
THREE

Capesthorne Capers

After a week or two, the gloomy cloud over Sydney passed and he became his old mischievous, teasing self again. However, Mary knew her jester would, at some point, be forced to wear the dark cloak of despair once more.

Apart from his down periods, when he only just managed to perform his duties, Sydney had the upper hand with the butler, who was at a loss to understand or manage this man. The butler even became wary of Sydney's quiet states; cautious in his handling, in case the "Jack" would spring from his box and wobble goggle-eyed to frighten him. Everyone knew time was on the butler's side, though, and it wasn't long before a badly timed, forced prank caused the joker to set alight to his own tail.

Sydney loved animals and they all loved him. He would stop to talk to any animals he and Mary came upon on their walks, be it stray dogs, cats, sheep or cows. He'd talk to them in a low, funny voice and they responded with friendly affection. The cats kept about the Hall for vermin control were his friends. When he spoke to them, they'd follow him around enjoying his company, brushing about his buckled shoes and white stockings. Although tolerated in most parts of the house, the cats were never allowed in the kitchen. Cat hairs, in carefully prepared food meant for aristocratic or royal diners, were a serious matter.

This day, however, a cat Sydney had been conversing with followed him into the kitchen. The normally quiet Fat Cook didn't miss anything that went on in her kitchen and was the first to spot the feline intruder. Exploding with rage, she boomed in a deep masculine voice, "Get that animal out of here. Out! Out! Out!", reaching a pitch that any fine baritone would have admired. Sydney admired it and he was only a keen amateur tenor.

Mary expected the blast from the Fat Cook to be devastating, for she had witnessed such events before and likened the Fat Cook to one of the round, fused, black bombs in comic cartoons. The fuse had been lit and the fat, round thing exploded.

Everyone but Sydney, stunned by the blast, chased the frightened creature around and over the large preparation table, the cat leading the race after at least three circuits. By this time, the excited pursuers had gained the enthusiasm of hounds after a fox, and the cat, coming upon the familiar buckled shoes and white stockings, clawed its way into the sanctuary of Sydney's arms.

Faced with a clawing cat and a baying mob, Sydney quickly disposed of the cat by dumping it in the open service lift, which he'd been standing by. He pulled the cord, sending the quarry to the safety of who knows where . . . The servants all knew it was to the Mistress's private quarters, and she hated cats.

The enquiry was thorough, and the authority generous enough to give Sydney a week's notice. Even this was too long for the puzzled butler.

Mary, full of anxiety over Sydney's fate, soon found the time to speak to him about it. What would he do? Where would he go? Sydney, currently being in his confident, comic mood, took it all as a joke. Mary didn't think it funny. She had backed this man and hoped for a future with him.

Sydney didn't seem at all concerned. Since leaving the Army at nineteen, he'd joined the thousands of maimed and scarred men that drifted job to job and place to place, begging and sleeping rough. He had short periods of employment; clerking, barman, waiting and, for a while, had even preached the Christian gospel from a soapbox on Hyde Park corner. Being on the road again held no fear for him.

Mary, though, with eyes on their future and the possibility of starting a family, persuaded him to apply to one of the ex-service welfare charities which had started up after the war in order to help the aimless drifting men. Some of these charities owned large estates and formed self-sufficient communities, with small factories and houses to give the men both job and home security. Sydney promised he would apply and Mary accepted that if he did, it would be a sign of his commitment to her.

On the day that Sydney left the hall, as many of the staff that could be in the kitchen to see him off did so.

He was dressed smartly in his mid-grey suit and highly polished shoes, his only other possessions in a small, brown, leather suitcase. The butler was there too, probably to make sure he left.

All the girls were teary and, as a final act of comedy, Sydney held the butler, kissed him on both cheeks, French style, and muttered something in a foreign tongue, possibly Indian and probably rude. This cheered everyone up; even the butler forced a smile and had to brush away a small tear.

Sydney left by the back door of the kitchen and crunched down the gravel path towards the tradesman's entrance, not turning to wave. The bright, bright rebel had left their lives.

It was weeks before Mary received a letter from Sydney, and she had not been her industrious, chatty self in all that time. The other servants understood; the entire household missed Sydney.

CHAPTER
FOUR

Drifting On

He had travelled to London, walking much of the way, and there located a charity which had an estate in Leatherhead, Surrey. They gave him a job in the market garden, a single man's lodgings and a wage of 30 shillings per week. Mary was pleased Sydney had obtained some security, but could they marry on that wage? And when could she see him? Leatherhead was 200 miles away.

She wrote to him of her concerns and his reply gave her more hope. The charity, the Ex-Services Welfare Society, was building cottages on the estate for families, and married men were paid more money. But still, when would she be able to see him? This problem was solved the following August of 1929, when Mary and a small number of servants would accompany Mrs Bromley-Davenport and other family members to their seaside home at Rustington, Sussex, only 40 miles from Leatherhead.

Sydney cycled to Rustington and called at the house without notice. He propped his bike against the back fence, crept up to the kitchen windows and jumped up like a Jack-in-the-Box to surprise Mary, who was at the sink looking out. Her heart thumped in her chest, and opening the back door, she scolded him, saying, "You fool, anyone could have been in here with me, do you want me to get the sack too?" She soon forgave him and was calmed by the long, firm hug he gave her, both not caring who would catch them.

Sydney stayed around the area for weeks, sleeping rough and sneaking in the kitchen for food. This was Mary's domain, the Fat Cook remaining at the Hall. It seemed the charity where Sydney resided was tolerant of the comings and goings of the inmates, and sympathetic to their needs, as he'd been free to leave and could return when his mission had been accomplished.

After a month, he prepared to return. Before he left, he produced a ring and asked Mary to marry him. Of course, she accepted, but had concerns with regards to finances, Sydney's illness and the differences of their religions. She was a Roman Catholic, although church attendance only meant a reason to leave the confines of the house for an hour or two, and Sydney was a Protestant. Her church would require that all their children — and there might be many due to the church not allowing birth control — be brought up as Roman Catholics.

Sydney would willingly sign up to this, not realising the burdens and responsibilities it would bring them both. The Anglican high church, which Sydney had attended all his life, had given him a strong moral conscience. He kept his word, didn't curse or swear and was probably a virgin when he married Mary. "Almost a Catholic", Mary would proudly say.

They married in July 1930 at the Church of Our Lady of Compassion, Willesden. Mary had given long notice of her leaving to the Hall, for she held an important post and the family and job had served her well for eleven years. It had given her confidence, status and security. She also loved living in a grand house, albeit in some of its furthest and darkest corners. And where better could she have observed the British aristocracy and grow to love them just a little.

They loved her and on her departure, she was piled with wedding gifts of linen, cutlery, china and glass. These came from both the staff and the Master and Mistress. She was given so much, that she accepted a lift to her lodgings in Willesden by Mr Bromley-Davenport when attending his duties as a Member of Parliament. Mary, of course, had to ride in the front with the chauffeur, and she gave a royal wave to the teary staff as she left the hall in grand style. Carefully cradled under her arm was the picture of Michael Collins, secreted in many wrapping of brown paper.

Her lodgings in Willesden were with a friend, Nellie Hicks, who had left Capesthorne Hall to marry two years earlier. Nellie was also Irish, and she had befriended Mary in the years at the Hall when Mary first entered service as a frightened sixteen-year-old. They were close friends and Nellie, her husband and two of their neighbours were the only ones to attend Sydney and Mary's wedding.

Sydney had arranged lodgings for them, paying 5 shillings a week for a room in a house in Skinners Lane, Ashtead, about a mile from Milner House, the estate of the charity where he worked. Moving here was to be the honeymoon, for there were no spare funds for anything fancier than that.

Their landlady, a widow, was a sombre soul and old before her time. Forty-five and childless, she had nursed her husband until he died as a result of the wounds he sustained during the First World War. Her own misery meant she was intolerant of their comings and goings and the noise, however quiet they were. Mary was sympathetic with her, Sydney less so, finding his habits of wit, charm and tease cut no ice with this sad lady.

Within weeks, Mary discovered she was pregnant. This delighted her, of course, but Sydney sank into a state of doom and gloom. He hadn't been able to charm the landlady and their tenure was precarious. The widow wouldn't allow them to stay with a child. It was not as though the lodgings were suitable; they had an oblong room, 15′ by 18′, containing a double bed, a table, four chairs, a wardrobe, dressing table and basic cooking facilities, with use of a bathroom and toilet across the hall.

However, the place was conveniently situated within walking distance of Sydney's work, and surrounded by many large houses where Mary had found a few cleaning jobs. The wages for scrubbing and cleaning were low and Mary could only find the occasional higher paid cooking job as a relief or temporary. They were able to save a little money each week and Mary would often repeat, as the coins clanked into the tin:

"Every little helps, the old woman said as she peed in the sea".

This failed to cheer Sydney up though. He worried and couldn't get enthusiastic about the baby. He also knew the cottages on the estate weren't ready and that he had little chance of obtaining one. This was because he'd told the doctor assessing the hospitalised soldiers that he'd suffered from depression before he joined up, and so received no pension.

Mary took this news badly. For many subsequent years of struggle, she'd reproach him for not having claimed a pension. After all, the battles he'd experienced in India couldn't have done his nerves much good, she reasoned.

They worried together through the months of the pregnancy, but when their son Geoffrey Harold was born in April 1931, their concerns lifted. Even the landlady cheered up and was prepared to let them stay on in the room and keep the large baby pram in the shed in the back garden. The baby weighed 6½ lbs; blue eyed like his father but dark haired like his mother. He was a quiet, contented child which was just as well, for his parents didn't want to upset the landlady.

Geoffrey was named after Sydney's younger brother, a nervy, artistic and slightly built lad who Sydney had fought hard to protect from the tough children of the fishing families around Hastings where they had grown up. Harry, or Harold, was Sydney's father's name.

Mary never understood why he bothered to acknowledge his family by naming the child after them. His family hadn't attended their wedding and had ignored the couple since the event, not forgiving Sydney for "going off and marrying this Irish woman". Neither did Sydney respect his father much; he thought him lazy, a malingerer, and believed he could have been something better than the postman he was. He also thought he spent too much time at the pub, getting drunk.

Geoffrey Harold had their names, but would not reflect any of the characteristics of his namesakes.

Things settled for a while, and Mary enjoyed pushing the baby around in the pram during the summer months. She was able to hold on to a few cleaning jobs, which meant that once again the savings box would ring with the dropping of the odd coin or two. The cooking jobs were out, however, as they would require too much of her attention to mind a baby. Her dusting, scrubbing and cleaning skills had held her in good stead and her employers were reluctant to lose her services.

Too much happiness and frolicking that summer led to another pregnancy, and once again they fell into the cycle of worry and insecurity. Surely their time had run out as far as the landlady was concerned ... The landlady did mellow a little and gave them until after the baby was born to vacate the room.

CHAPTER
FIVE

Aunt Bridget

Mary's mother, Bridget, had never contacted her directly throughout all the years she worked at Capesthorne Hall. Any news would come through John and Rose. This was because it couldn't be acknowledged in the household that Bridget and Mary were mother and daughter.

Bridget knew all about the progress that Mary had made, through the discreet questioning of the staff that had cause to be at the Macclesfield or London home, namely the valet and chauffeur. She was very pleased with her daughter but grew concerned when informed that Mary had left the hall to marry "this smart but reckless young man", as the valet put it. Bridget traced the young couple, via Nellie Hicks, to Ashtead, and one day took the 40-minute train journey down from London and turned up at the house.

Mary and Sydney were out walking, with the baby in the pram. When the landlady opened the front door, she was taken aback by the tall, serious, authoritative figure clad in black standing on the step, asking to see Mary. She thought the lady must be a nun, and sensed she'd had an unhappy life. She never hesitated to let her wait in the young couple's room. The cot in the room told the old lady that she had a grandchild, bringing both a smile to her lips and tears to her eyes. She sat happy and wept, and dwelt on what might have been.

When the walkers returned, Mary greeted her mother coldly, as if to say, "What are you doing here?" Sydney, however, was pleased to meet his mother-in-law, shaking her hand and hugging her. He warmed the icy atmosphere between mother and daughter by remarking that the landlady must have thought the "Angel of Death" had arrived when she appeared on the doorstep. It wasn't long before the grandmother was holding the baby and they were all enjoying a cup of tea.

Mary took years to warm towards her mother and always called her by her Christian name. Bridget must have longed to be called mother. Sydney was always friendly towards Bridget and curbed the mother-in-law jokes accordingly. She liked him very much, needing an ally in the camp.

Bridget couldn't fail to be thrilled by the pretty model of a grandson, but was shocked to discover her daughter was again pregnant, and that they had to leave their lodgings within months. She left the house worrying about the plight of the young couple and as she walked with Sydney to the train station, she promised she'd do something to help them.

Within days a letter arrived from Bridget, offering to give them £400 to buy a cottage. Mary was reluctant to accept, but Sydney argued that it was their only hope of

25

owning a house, as they didn't stand a chance on his wage of £2 a week. They accepted and had the excitement of finding a terraced cottage at 37 Caenwood Road, Ashtead, just a mile away near Leatherhead, by the railway line and woods.

The cottage was one of a pair built in 1903 for brickworkers, grandly named "May Villas". The left one, No. 35 Caenwood Road, was where the Cullens lived and the Browns resided on the right in No. 37. Further cottages were built in 1904, and Nos. 39, 41, 43, 45 housed the Adams, the Osbornes, the Jupps and Granny Overton respectively.

The cottage design was basic, two rooms downstairs — the front and the back rooms — and two bedrooms above these. From the front door, a lino covered passage led to a door to the back room, past a door to the front room and stairs to the bedrooms on the right. At the back of each cottage, half the width of the back room, was the scullery or kitchen, a pantry and an outside toilet.

Above these was a small box room in which a single bed would fit. A tin bath hung on a nail on the wall in the backyard, ready to be lifted in for bath nights. The back room had an old black cast-iron range for cooking and water heating, and the front room and bedrooms all had black cast-iron open fires. Electric lighting had been put in, but the glass-domed and mantled gas lighting was still in place and usable.

Mary and Sydney were excited to be buying a house of their own after the periods of anxiety they had gone through, but slow conveyancing meant they'd still be in lodgings when their second son, Michael George, was born in 1932.

Michael was named in honour of Mary's Irish hero Michael Collins, but Sydney's contribution of the name of England's patron saint more than compensated. Although the choice was probably because Sydney's paternal grandfather was a William George.

Boy number two weighed just over 7 lbs and had his father's hair colour and blue eyes. He was a loud, demanding, noisy baby and if he wasn't, he certainly might have been the reason for the exodus from the lodgings.

On the day of the move, Mary pushed the pram containing the two babies while Sydney carried their immediate supplies and they walked to take possession of No. 37. Sydney then used the pram to return and transport the rest of their belongings, including the picture of Michael Collins, making five trips in all.

Number 37 was 150 yards on the left into Caenwood Road, the total length of the road being about 300 yards. On the right at the top of the road was a piece of wasteland that ran down to the back gardens into Oakhill Road, which joined Caenwood Road about halfway down.

The first dwellings on the left into Caenwood Road were a pair of semi-detached Edwardian houses. The first of these had a very large garden and many outbuildings and corrugated tin garages, with a driveway that led out onto Barnett Wood Lane. The lane was the main road and bus route from Lower Ashtead to Leatherhead.

27

Following on from the Edwardian semis were a group of old cottages, about twelve in all, the last of which had been turned into a corner shop. It sold mainly food, sweets and soft drinks, but also a few small domestic items such as soap and first aid and sewing items.

Next to the shop was a piece of wasteground which would have been big enough to build two more cottages, but was the access drive to the back gardens of all the cottages from the top of the road down to number 45. Next to the wasteground, and following on from the shop, were numbers 35 and 37.

The remainder of the lower end of the road, on both sides, were semis built in the 1930s. These had indoor bathrooms and toilets. This end of the road, a cul-de-sac which finished at the railway line, was referred to as the "posh" end.

CHAPTER
SIX

Room to Breed

Mary threw herself enthusiastically into the arranging and cleaning of the house. She still managed to keep some of her domestic jobs and saved to buy furniture. The start was a double bed, the cot, the pram and a few orange boxes for seats. The picture of Michael Collins found pride of place on the wall in the back room.

The toil did not help Mary's health. In the late autumn she had a miscarriage, another boy. She claimed it to have been brought on when she was running to catch a bus. Devastated by her loss, she arranged for a proper burial of the child in the area for Catholics at St Mary's Church, Leatherhead.

She took months to recover from the trauma, but by June 1933 the child production line was once again operational. William Cyril was born in February 1934. His mother's waters broke at the top of the stairs of No. 37, which she'd been cleaning, and she crawled into the back bedroom, into the double bed which she and Sydney shared. Someone was sent by bike to fetch the midwife, and when she arrived William had already been born and was contentedly sucking on his mother's leg.

Apart from his dramatic entrance into the world, William was an easygoing child and would not disrupt the household too much. "William" had been a compromise in the choice of name; it was Sydney's grandfather's name, as well as the brother of Uncle John in Ireland. February 9th, the day William Cyril was born, is St Cyril's day, but this name was seldom mentioned, particularly in a road which had justly earned the title "Do-as-you-like Street". William would remain neutral in both looks and leanings towards either the shamrock or the crown. He had his father's light-coloured, wispy hair and blue eyes, but his mother's delicate facial features.

When Sydney was well, he was able to help Mary in the handling of the three boys and took on one or two gardening jobs at the larger houses in nearby lanes in his spare time. The little money he earned helped support his growing family.

Geoffrey, now nearly four, was given small jobs to help his mother and particularly the caring of Michael. The fetching and carrying jobs he did, he did thoroughly and well and with his good looks, Sydney likened him to a little servant and teasingly named him "Jane". He found his younger brother, Michael, who by this time was almost his equal in size, a little harder to handle. Their many boyhood scuffles honed Geoffrey sufficiently so that in his teens he became a schoolboy champion boxer for Surrey.

Sydney stopped using Jane as a nickname early on and helped Geoffrey and Michael to learn to box. Sydney had boxed while he was in the Army, but it was unlikely that the tactics he demonstrated to the boys would have been valid while he was in the ring. When sparring with his tiny opponents, he'd hold his left-gloved hand in the air and twist it, causing the youngster to look up, only to tap them on the face or tummy with his right hand.

When Sydney and Mary moved to Caenwood Road, far removed from the posh and strict formality of Capesthorne Hall, they dropped their full Christian names and became "Syd and May". The boys were given nicknames. "Jane" was not suitable for a tough little fighter and so Geoffrey became "Brownie". Michael became Mick, which always seemed sufficient, and, because of his keenness to play with the buttons from the button tin, William became "Buttons". This later changed to "Buster", a title more suiting a clever, witty and charming little lad. The full Christian names would only surface in formal, serious or angry situations. Mary and Syd doted on their three healthy, pretty children, always at play with them and taking them for walks, with Mary lovingly comforting them if they should fall.

During the summer months, fund-raising fêtes and garden parties were held at Milner House, the estate where Syd worked. Mary loved to take the boys and welcomed the opportunity to put on her best dress. These events, often attended by royalty, would also be a reminder of the happy years she'd spent at Capesthorne Hall. Syd would attend, but only in his capacity as a demonstrator of the charity's work. This might be ploughing, planting, or picking vegetables and tomatoes for market. He'd had enough of dressing up.

When she could, Bridget would travel down from London, bringing small gifts and sweets for the boys and a little money to help the family finances. Not always happy with these visits, Mary liked the children to call the dark-clad lady "Aunt Bridget", not grandma. However loving and big-hearted Mary was, she found it hard to embrace and accept her mother.

When Buster's first birthday was celebrated, it was a double event, for Mary believed she was pregnant again. She was right and in September 1935, Stanley James was born, the names being drawn from a selection placed in a hat. Although his birth weight was average, he would not grow into the fat, bonny, bouncing child his brothers had. He was grizzly and moody which led to his first nickname of "Bagpipes". which soon changed to "Skinny" and then evolving to "Flint", a name that remained with him until well into his teens.

The burdens on Mary were increasing as fast as the family grew. She would carefully balance the budget by her philosophy of "looking after the pennies and the pounds will look after themselves". She had a little tally book with the corner shop at No. 29; she or one of the boys collected groceries and odds and ends on a daily basis as she needed them, paying off the total a little each week.

Her cooking skills gave her economic use of limited resources; she could have made a meal out of old boot leather. Syd grew fruit and vegetables in the garden or brought them from the places where he worked. Occasionally he'd bring home a pigeon, rabbit or pheasant that had been shot as pest control in the market gardens. Mary was accomplished at preparing and cooking these and they'd provide a real feast day. Hot stews with dumplings, roasts, steamed sweet puddings, bread puddings and sponges were the staples, nothing was wasted. Mary was very much at home with the black range and never had to resort to cooking boot leathers.

Syd fared worse. Every few months he would sink into a depressed state, remaining unapproachable for days. The children would wonder why Daddy wasn't funny and playful, why he just sat winding ravelled wool into a ball and weeping. At least his job was safe, and Mary would support them all with her boundless energy.

Brownie would be starting school the following spring; budgeting would have to provide money for the regulation grey short trousers and white shirt, as well as new shoes and socks. There was no Catholic school close by for the children to attend, so they'd attend the state school one mile away towards Ashtead Railway Station.

Mary walked young Brownie to school, Buttons and Bagpipes in the pram and Mick trotting alongside, taunting his elder brother in his smart new clothes. They made a noisy group, joining all the other mums, babies and kids on their way to school. After a few accompanied trips, Brownie joined the trail on his own, being the first one of the family launched into the big wide world.

Mick, still dressed in the hand-me-downs from his big brother, resented Brownie's smart new outfit and made it a reason to pick a fight on his return from school. He waited at the top of the road and Brownie, never one to stand down from a fight, took him on. They scuffled on the grassy wasteland near the bus stop at the top of the road for what seemed like hours to the little combatants, but was actually only minutes. They were stopped by an old man getting off the bus who with a shout sent them scurrying home.

The few minutes scuffle was enough to collect grassy smudges and dust on their clothes; they were in for a scolding. Mary was tough on discipline and after a loud telling off, the boys got a hard whack on the backs of their legs. She didn't try to discover the rights and wrongs of the matter. It was expedient to blame them both, dish out the punishment and get on with the added chores of cleaning and mending their clothes. Bagpipes and Buttons looked on from the pram and couldn't wait to join in with all the excitement.

Mary worried about the danger the toddlers faced with the range, which always seemed to carry a kettle or cooking pot. It was solid fuel-fired, either coke or coal or, as Syd thought, bits of wood, fir-cones and small pieces of rubber he picked up. Mary never wanted the little ones too near and to make them aware of the danger, she'd take their hands and lightly burn them on the front.

It seemed Syd's unintended method of teaching respect for the fire worked just as well, for as he piled some of his flammable material on, the chimney would roar with the flames and it was easy to convince a small child that a monster lived there. The kidding abruptly stopped on the occasions when the chimney caught fire and there'd be a panicked attempt to stop it by cutting off the air supply to the range. When some new furniture was bought, the orange boxes, having served as seats until then, had made the monster roar.

As the boys grew, they were encouraged to walk longer and further to different playsites and picnic areas. The pram was always pushed containing a child or two and would serve as a lift should any of the toddlers' legs tire. Young friends from the street would often tag along too, their parents always pleased to be rid of them. The groups might contain ten or twelve people, adults and children, and they'd walk to a site for a swim or picnic, sometimes up to four miles from home.

Some of the places visited on walks would include Ashtead Woods and the ponds at Epsom, Oxshott Woods and common or the Black Pond at Esher.

But a trip to the water meadows beside the River Mole at Leatherhead was the favourite of everyone. On hot summer days the whole family, plus their friends, would walk the two miles to the river for a picnic and swim. The route took the party past Prewett's dairy and farm, where they heard the steady thump, thump, thump of the diesel engine driving the milking

35

machine, and smelt the warm aroma of the cow pats on the hot road surface leading to the milking parlour.

They'd be within two hundred yards downhill, to the river and meadows, where the cows had been grazing. The party would quicken the pace, the elder boys racing ahead to the river and, without settling to a picnic site in the vast rough-grassed area, they'd throw off their clothes and jump into the icy water. Their swimming costumes already on, no time was wasted and their clothes would be left scattered on the river bank.

Mary and Syd would select a picnic site and play area free from ants, wasps and cowpats, with the grass fairly short for games. It wouldn't be too far from a hedge where the wood was collected for a fire. Brewing the tea was a must for Mary and Syd. When the swimmers were tired and hungry, they'd find the adults and feast on sandwiches, cakes and squash. When they'd recovered from the swim, the games would start, and after this hot, exhausting round of games, another cool swim was needed.

These were very hot, tiring days out, and when it was time to make the long trek back home, there were arguments among the children as to who would hitch a ride on the pram carrying the young ones. But Syd and Mary never had the luxury of a lift, and stoically carried their burdens home to their beds.

Mary also took the boys on train and bus trips as they grew older. She took them, two at a time, to London to visit the museums, Madame Tussauds, Trafalgar Square or the zoo, often ending with tea at a

Lyons Corner House. Mick managed to get himself lost on a trip to London Zoo, and was given a bun and left at the first aid station until his anxious mother was able to find him. Sometimes in London, she would take the children to visit "Aunt Bridget".

Although Mary didn't attend church regularly ("too busy, God will understand"), she had all children baptised into the Catholic Church. Syd had agreed to this before he and Mary married. She did, though, encourage the boys to go to church; they attended St Peter's Church at Leatherhead, which was nearer to Caenwood Road than the Catholic Church in Ashtead. The boys were suitably trained and disciplined by the church, becoming altar servers and choir boys, going to church up to three times on a Sunday.

It was through the church that Mary found her first "needy" family. These were the Calagans, another embryonic Catholic tribe in the making. There was father, mother, a toddler, a baby in the pram and they were homeless. Big-hearted Mary offered them the front room of No. 37. It was empty at the time and underused.

Ten people then resided in the house. It was cramped and noisy, tempers flared and after tolerating it for a few months, Syd on this rare occasion put his foot down and insisted the Calagans left. It was a sad sight to see the family trudge away, children and possessions in the pram, towards their new-found lodgings in Epsom. Mary felt their pain. Syd justified his stand, keeping the place for his family which was still growing. Another baby was due in the November of that year, 1937.

Surprise, surprise, it was another boy, named Frederick after Syd's elder brother, with the second name Alexander. They were fast running out of suitable boys names. The lad was tiny, only 5 lbs in weight. A teacup would have made an oversized hat for the child, Mary observed. She also thought that turning babies out this small might be heralding the end of her breeding programme.

What nutrition the child had failed to obtain from the womb, he quickly gained from his mother's milk as well as from the bits and pieces fed to him by his four interested siblings. The newest family member grew fast, and within a couple of years was as big as Bagpipes, who he liked to fight, earning him the nickname "Scrapper".

CHAPTER
SEVEN

Patriotic Passions

The picture of Mary's hero Michael Collins, hanging on the wall in the back room, always reminded her of the bitter struggles the Irish had had against the hated Black and Tans, and her boys would know of that history.

The lesson would begin with the baby being bounced on her knee to a jig; "Dee, diddle diddle diddle, diddle diddle dee". The boys would join in and press their mother for "Paddy Maginty's Goat", and as the emotion swelled, Mary's eyes would fill with tears. The rebel choir progressed to "The Wearing of the Green" and on to the defiant marching of "Soldiers Are We Whose Lives Are Pledged To Ireland". Mary produced many rebels, but none that were prepared to sacrifice their lives for Ireland. The hypocrisy of the Catholic Church, their English upbringing and a liberal, tolerant father saw to that.

Syd's habit of teasing could easily raise Mary's anger or "get her goat up" as she would say, and she was particularly vulnerable over the plight of her homeland. Arguments would flare up and as well as swear words and blasphemies, remarks from Mary would include

"I'll swing for you, you bleeder" or "I'll dance on your grave".

Syd would tease her to further inflame her anger with, "Well, they're not my kids". He carefully calculated the effect of his words and knew at what point missiles would fly across the room at him, and that if he stood near the picture of Michael Collins, it would inhibit her aim. She wouldn't have hit that. Syd's boxing training had stood him in good stead, the bobbing and weaving meant he never got hit.

As the worries grew, Mary's temper flared with the boys as well and the occasional item was thrown, often missing, but Mick was unfortunate enough to have a tin mug thrown at him, because "he had the devil in him", which cut his head. Mary was full of remorse and hugged him firmly.

Syd didn't keep his teasing exclusively for Mary, he also teased the boys. If, after an hour or two of rough playing outside, they returned tired and hungry to ask Dad where Mum was, he'd reply "Gawn awf with a soldier", or "Gawn awf with the milkman". He knew Mary was only at a neighbour's house, having a chat and a cup of tea. If the boys came home with a cut finger or grazed leg, his call for a saw to "cut it awf" soon stopped the crying.

With a bunch of mischievous boys, hardly a day went by without some form of injury, a cut, a graze, a sting, a thorn or a bump on the head. Mary would exclaim "Oh! Jesus, Mary and Joseph, what has the child done now?"

She was full of ideas and home remedies to fix injuries, as doctors cost money. Cuts and grazes were thoroughly scrubbed and washed. If the whole child needed a scrub, the tin bath was lifted from the wall in the back yard, placed in front of the range, filled with hot water and one or all of the boys would be dumped in. The scrubbing of the wound or the water being too hot was far worse than the pain of the injury, the boys quickly learnt not to mention anything other than serious injuries.

If a splinter or wound did turn septic, out would come a needle from the sewing basket, dipped in boiling water and thrust into the infected area, with peroxide poured on. The wound would sting sharply and bubble away the germs causing the infection, but if it did persist, a hot bread poultice made from stale bread and boiling water was slapped over the wound and held there for a few minutes. Both of these methods were painful as Mary was never very good with a needle and had no way of accurately judging the heat of the poultice.

A sting would be bathed in vinegar or rubbed with a dock leaf, a thorn dug out with a needle, and a bump on the head meant a dunking under the cold water tap. If a wound formed a scab, the boys were constantly reminded, "It will never get well if you pick it."

The children caught all the common childhood diseases and passed them on to each other; it was at these times the doctor was consulted and the proper medicines purchased and administered. The weakness in the health of the boys appeared to be with their ears and throat, and three at different times were hospitalised to have their tonsils removed. The ear-aches were soothed when Mary poured warm oil into the ear and plugged it with cotton wool. As a relief for a "chesty cawf", Mary prepared a bowl of boiling water laced with vaporising oil, the child stood or sat with his head over the steaming bowl covered with a towel or blanket. This exercise made their noses run, their eyes sting and loosened the phlegm on their chests.

The workload, the finances and Syd's black periods were wearing Mary down. She became short-tempered, swore and blasphemed and when she could budget for it, fortified herself with Guinness. But she was resilient and much needed by her family; she did not stay down for long. She couldn't, another child was on the way and in April 1939, Patrick Eamon was born.

A ten pounder, fair haired and blue eyed, Mary had got her little Irishman and firmly stamped him with two Irish names to prove it. When a new baby arrived in the family, the child, in this case Fred, that had the privilege of sleeping in a cot in the back bedroom where Mum and Dad slept, was moved into the front bedroom with the other boys. The front bedroom already looked like a crowded barrack room with four iron framed beds, and would now have to make room for Fred's cot or another bed for him.

Mary needed another source of income, Syd's low wage and casual earnings would not suffice, and she persuaded him that another lodger for the front room would help. A blind lady, Miss Axe, and her companion, again found through church contacts, moved in. A little extra money could be earned by Mary supplying and cooking their meals and they would hardly hear the old ladies. The old ladies heard the boys in the room above, though; you couldn't stop boys picking fights on the soft landing sites of beds with pillows as handy, impressive, explosive weapons. The old ladies couldn't tolerate the noise for more than a few weeks and left.

At this point, the church elders became interested in the family, in which there were 6 boys, assuming there must be the makings of a priest there somewhere. Two men in dark suits visited the house, viewed the chaos and negotiated with Syd in low tones. They left agreeing to supply a little money each week to help with food and clothing.

Mary had not entered into the talks with the men because her strict, Catholic upbringing in Ireland where priests and men of the church held the power made her fear them. On this occasion Syd felt a particular responsibility, for unbeknownst to Mary, the previous winter he had turned down help from the Ex-Services Welfare Society of a winter fuel payment amounting to 25% of his wage.

When the credit on the little tally book with the corner shop had reached its limit or if they didn't sell the goods Mary needed, she would send one of the boys down Barnett Wood Lane to the shops near the Plough Roundabout. The journey was about a mile and the road wasn't busy at that time, so it was safe for even very young children to walk it alone. Down the lane on the right was a large open field, on the far side of which was an area known as the "dump", and on the left was a twenty-acre coppice of hazel, oak and ash.

If the boys were otherwise engaged, footballing, cricketing or fighting, they could refuse the errand but would be reproached by Mary with "All right, little apples will grow again". These words were suitably confusing and frightening to young boys, and could have been a witch or gypsy curse for all they knew, but a bribe always followed, of a penny for some sweets, and an errand boy was selected.

Granny Smith's shop was the first shop down Barnett Wood Lane, just past the farm on the left. The shop was owned and run by Granny Smith and her husband, and never started out to be a shop at all. It was a low lean-to shed attached to the side of their cottage, and from the 1900s had been a destination and refreshment point for the hoards of cyclists peddling out of smoky London on fine weekends in spring and summer.

It was still isolated and although the golden age of the cyclists had passed, there was still evidence about the place that they had been. There was a small off-road parking area at the front of the shop where one could imagine stacks of resting bikes. There were many enamelled advertising signs tempting the tired cyclists to fortify themselves. On the left and next to the front door to the shop was a gateway to the tea garden and in the garden were the time-worn and moss-covered remains of tables and chairs once used by the cyclists. The garden had been an orchard and one very old pear tree grew in the hedge next to the lane, a good source of fruit for the boys if they visited the shop in the autumn.

Granny Smith looked like Mrs Punch in glasses and it took some courage for a small boy to give his order, when his head only just reached the top of the advertisement-clad counter. The shop was crammed with goods, many hanging from the ceiling, and although Granny Smith's head avoided them, when her husband came from the back room to serve, he had to stoop and dodge. Granny Smith was kind and patient, her husband less so. She would bend her ear close to the counter so she could take the whispered order from the small boy.

One autumn, Mick, the errand boy, having made his purchase including his sweet as reward, decided to stop and pick up some fallen pears in the lane and while busily collecting the fruit, he was knocked over by a man on a bike coming down the lane. (This may have been a cyclist refusing to believe that his era had passed.) The man dusted the lad down and gave him 6d compensation, which Mick used to buy a Lyons Fruit Pie at the shop. The man also got his rest and refreshment, as Mrs Punch was very kind to all.

Further down the lane from Granny Smith's, was the Plough Roundabout, and on the outer edges were a number of shops including a butcher's shop, a ladies hairdresser and a combined grocery store and Post Office.

An occasional errand to the Post Office to cash or buy a postal order would be carried out by one of the boys. Mr Anderson, the owner of the shop, was an intimidating figure to a small lad, who looked up from below the high counter to see this fuzzy-haired and squared-jawed man with the gravelly voice behind the grill.

More often than not, though, the trip to the Plough Roundabout was to the Plough Pub, after which the roundabout was named. This was to fetch a bottle of Guinness or old ale. The pub was on the opposite side of the roundabout to the shops. These trips occurred about the end of September when Mary decided it was time to make Christmas pudding, and the puddings would need time to mature. The selected child carried a bag of empty beer bottles to retrieve the money to help pay for the beer, or one of the quart bottles might be refilled again from the old ale pump in the bar.

Children were not allowed in pubs, but they were allowed to collect alcohol from a small, private entrance and room called an off-licence. The counter in the off-licence was very high and if there was too much noisy chatter and laughter in the public and lounge bars either side, the publican would not know if anyone had entered the off-licence. He might have occasionally glanced around into the space, but missed the tired little lad hugging the bag of empties below the level of the high counter.

At this point, the child had two options to ensure that he got noticed: he could wait for an adult to come in to be served, or for a lull in the noise from the bars and then he would open and close the heavy entrance door with a bang. Having gained attention, the empties were lifted to the counter, computed, money passed over and purchases made.

The child would then haul the full bottles on the mile journey back up the lane, making sure that none were broken on the way. How much of the old ale or Guinness was used in the puddings and how much was consumed by Mary was never known, but they were exceedingly good puddings.

CHAPTER
EIGHT

War Torn

As if Mary's worries weren't enough, the autumn of 1939 saw the start of the Second World War. At first, it seemed nothing was happening, except that all the youths and younger married men left the street and went away to join the services. However, within weeks, there was a sudden rush of activity, government directives and recommendations to comply with.

Everybody's windows had to be totally blacked out at night as lights seen would help enemy bombers sight their targets. It was recommended that windows were criss-crossed with tape to stop a blast shattering the glass, scattering razor-sharp shards to kill or maim.

Air raid shelters were hurriedly built and either buried underground, built of brick above ground or supplied in kit form as a table shelter. The school the boys attended had an underground air raid shelter built. It was long and humped, looking like an ancient burial mound from the outside. Inside, it was dark and damp, there were bench seats either side and duckboards down the middle. The duckboards were needed because water would collect in the bottom and frogs would hop and swim about. Seemingly they too liked to shelter from the bombs.

People who could afford the labour or had enough energy themselves would dig out and build their own shelters in their gardens. Many of the people at the lower end of the street did this. An above ground shelter was built on the piece of wasteland at the top of the street, where Brownie and Mick had one of their many scuffles a few years ago.

For most people in the cottages, including the Browns, a table shelter was the best option but only if the room was big enough to fit it in. The shelter was the size of a large kitchen table and consisted of four chunky angle irons for legs, a great, heavy steel sheet for the top, with the underneath caged by a thick wire mesh. A gap in the mesh was left for access to the shelter underneath and the whole thing was put together with large nuts and bolts. At No. 37, the table shelter was put up in the centre of the back room, and took up about a third of the space, replacing the wooden table, which was stored outside until the war ended.

At night when the wailing sirens warned of an air raid and the pumping boom boom of the ack ack guns started, with the long beams of the searchlights moving eerily across the sky, the family were shepherded from their beds and walked dreamily down the stairs to bunch up under the table. Many a bruise to toe, knee or head was caused by that sleepy walk and collision with the rusty shelter.

When the knot of moaning, half-awake kids got too much for Syd under the table, he took his chances in the cupboard under the stairs, and sometimes one or two of the boys would go with him. The cupboard was deep in unwanted articles and clothing; the boys felt safe buried there. But once, when a bomb on a daytime raid fell close by, the doors and frame shook with the blast.

When a daytime bombing raid occurred, the children who were out playing would have just a minute or two to reach a shelter, and Mary would not know if they were safe until the "All Clear" sounded and the children returned home.

All the worrying was left to Mum and Dad; the boys enjoyed the war. They were excited by the damage the bombs caused, and played in the bomb craters. They collected shell cases, bullets and bullet cases. They marvelled at the tin foil dropped by the enemy planes to confuse the radar, and kicked the occasional unexploded incendiary. They searched for the twisted, shattered shrapnel and if it was still warm, all the more exciting.

They loved the convoys of soldiers, the tanks, the motorbikes and lorries. If the soldiers were American or Canadian, they could cadge with a call, "Got any gum, chum?" and often got some too. They enjoyed watching the English fighter planes shoot down the enemy bombers, and cheered when a bomber crashed to earth. They watched in wonder the jumbo barrage balloons straining on their anchor wires and proudly carried their little boxes containing their gas masks.

When nothing much was happening, apart from the stray bomb or two dropping nearby, the boys preferred to remain in their bedrooms during night raids. From their window they could watch the waving beams of searchlights illuminating the barrage balloons and the sky over London lit up with fire, as though there was an early dawn. They heard the drone of the planes, the sound of the guns and the exploding bombs.

Aunt Bridget, up to this time, had been visiting the family once or twice a year, assisting them with gifts and money. Her visits were restricted by the war, when travel became difficult and dangerous and contact was lost. She was heard of no more and although Syd had tried to find her after the war, it was believed she had died in the severe bombing suffered by London. She must have been happier in her final years, for she was allowed to be called Grandma by her grandsons.

As well as the war, and the loss of her mother, Mary had other things on her mind at this time; she was pregnant again. In March 1941, while a daytime raid was taking place, she gave birth to a 9 lb baby girl and named her Thelma Josephine. Thelma was born in the double bed in the back bedroom, and the midwife came down the stairs to summon the boys to meet their baby sister.

They surrounded the bed and with wide-eyed, angelic faces peered in wonder at the little thing in the bed with Mum.

"What's a girl?" asked Patrick.

He would soon find out when he played Doctors and Nurses with the little girls from the street, as his elder brothers had done before him. At this moment though, he wondered how he would fit into the barrack room at the front, with his rough and tough brothers.

Mary was overjoyed at having a daughter, and was glad that the child had been born late in the family order, which prevented her from becoming a servant to all the males. She joked that the baby's arrival had caused the air raid and had spoilt her all-male football team she had hoped to produce.

CHAPTER
NINE

Full House

Mary didn't know it at the time, but Thelma would be the last child she would have. Her health was suffering and she was advised by both the midwife and doctor to practice some form of birth control. Syd was in favour of preventing any more pregnancies, and about this time he moved into a single bed, which had a deeply sunken mattress, in the box room. This room was accessed through the back bedroom and down a step. Thelma and Mary were left to share the back bedroom from here on, and as Mary's adherence to the church rules on birth control were solid, this move may have helped to limit the amorous activities of the couple.

Apart from the rearranging of the sleeping quarters, nothing much changed on Thelma's arrival. Up to three of the boys were scrubbed in the tin bath together and baby would fit in somewhere. But what was exciting for the boys was the "sleep-in" gas mask that their baby sister had. The family complete now totalled nine, Mum, Dad and seven children, their ages from the newborn baby Thelma to Brownie, who was nearly ten. The house and finances were at breaking point.

Syd's wicked humour continued, but at the time and in the circumstances of the war, his joking could have caused much trouble. If a friend of one of the boys had called at the house to play, Syd would ask, "How's your Mum?" and when he received the reply from the innocent boy, "All right," Syd would say "Tell her I'll be round." Whether these messages ever got back to the mums or not was never known, but Syd Brown at No. 37 with seven kids must have gained a reputation second only to the American and Canadian soldiers.

Mary enjoyed company and she would chat to the neighbours over the fence, out in the street or have two or three ladies in for a talk over a cup of tea. Phil Cullen from No. 35 and she might chat while hanging out the washing on the long lines running down the gardens.

Granny Osborne from No. 41 often sat with her feet stretched out on a long bench in her front garden and held court with the neighbours or people passing by. She watched her grandchildren and all the other children playing somewhere near the lamppost on the corner of Oakhill Road, the girls skipping or hopscotch and the boys' football or hoops, or just teasing the girls. The Doctors and Nurses games took place out of sight of the adults.

Another good friend of Mary's was Winnie Skinner. She lived in Oakhill Close, a cul-de-sac off Oakhill Road, containing about thirty pre-war semi-detached houses. The end houses all surrounded a long, grassed roundabout. Her husband, Ron, was a small man, but did a very hard job as a ganger, maintaining the railway track, keeping open his part of the railway network to support the war effort.

Winnie and Ron were a childless couple and were about ten years younger than Mary and Syd. Winnie would spend many hours at No. 37, admiring the children and talking to Mary. She envied Mary and her family and particularly liked the boys. She'd bounce the younger ones on her knee, but the older boys were caught by her, hugged and embarrassed by the red outline of her lips when she planted a big kiss on their face. Winnie was all lipstick, powder and perfume and gave the boys their first experience of a sweet-smelling, sexy woman, but they ran to avoid her grasp and quickly wiped off the lipstick.

Tessie Jupp from No. 43 Caenwood Road was another good friend to Mary and was a big person in every sense: big-hearted, big in body and big in personality. She loved her fur coats, fags and booze. Her favourite place was a smoky, noisy bar in a pub, and that was just the sort of atmosphere she and Mary created, on occasions, in the back scullery at No. 37.

Mary, intending to get the washing done in the old, steamy copper boiler, would get a visit from Tessie, arriving wide-eyed, frizzy-haired, a fag drooping from her mouth, carrying a bottle of gin or stout, carefully taking the step down into the steam-filled scullery. She would stand and drink, chat and smoke while Mary continued with the chores. They joked and laughed and shared one another's troubles; Tessie had many of her own. She was a few years older than Mary and had two teenage daughters to worry about, as well as a young son, Peter, who was a little older than Thelma.

The scullery "pub" was a dangerous place for children to enter when troubled, sentimental ladies were downing a bottle of gin; they risked a bear hug and a smouldering fag in their cheek, or the bribe of sixpence to sing a sentimental Irish song. Captured by the spirit and atmosphere of the occasion, Tessie wouldn't even leave the steamy, smoky room to visit the outside lavatory. She would simply pull out the white, enamelled washing bucket, squat on it and have her pee, enormous buttocks squashing over the edges.

When food and clothing were rationed and books of coupons issued, Mary claimed nine books, one for each member of the family. She was already running a very tight economy, managing by mending, adapting and accepting gifts of clothing and shoes, and handing down clothing from boy to boy. Her frugality when catering was second to none, and when she visited the grocers or butchers with a fistful of ration books, they would be pleased, at last, to cut off a large slice of butter, cheese or meat as they had done pre-war. The alcohol was rationed only by the money supply.

Mary was not very good at sewing, and the patches she put on trousers or jackets would cause more embarrassment than the holes they covered. They were always badly matched for colour, crooked and stitched in bright coloured thread. Her darning was appalling too and it was better for the boys to learn to do these jobs themselves, particularly the sewing-on of cub and scout achievement badges. Many an aspiration to be a sixer, seconder or patrol leader could have been dashed by a badly sewn or crookedly placed patch.

The boys learnt to sew and darn, but their Mum, their cooking teacher, was the best, and she confidently let them experiment in that department. They would be encouraged to help with the vegetable and fruit preparation and the preparing and mixing of puddings, pies, pastries and cakes. They'd busily fetch and carry the ingredients to the table, and stand and watch or help with the beating, stirring, mixing, peeling, cutting or shucking. The younger children spent most of their time eating the raw carrot, cabbage, fruit peelings and peas. The older children waited and negotiated, sometimes noisily, for the choice scrapings from the mixing bowls which had been used for the sponges, icing sugar and jams.

Christmas pudding-making time, at the end of September, was special, with a kaleidoscope of ingredients filling the table and the currants, raisins, sultanas, candied peel and dried fruit were the glistening rewards for the busy little workers. But nothing would start until the Guinness or old ale was collected, and who could be bribed to go, leaving all this excitement and all those rich tit-bits?

Syd wasn't very good at mending things either, when using his last and hammer to fix Blakies or studs to boots and shoes, the point of the stud often entered the inside of where the foot sat; a painful surprise to the wearer. The boys loved studs on their footwear and happily scuffed and sparked on roads and footpaths when noisily playing or making their way to school.

One of Syd's mending jobs went badly wrong when he fixed a doorknob to the scullery door. He simply held the brass knob on the bolt by putting a small nail through existing holes in the neck of the knob and the bolt. The problem was that the pointed end of the nail was protruding and waiting to be gripped by an unsuspecting victim. In this case, it was poor Mary, who spent much of her time in and out of the scullery, seemingly endlessly washing clothes. Mary had gripped the doorknob hard and the protruding nail entered the index finger of her right hand. The nail was rusty and dirty, having been retrieved from Syd's stock of fixings in an old wooden box.

Mary didn't take enough care of herself and when the wound went septic and the poultice and peroxide didn't work, the pain became unbearable and she consulted a doctor. With the proper treatment, the finger was saved, but the nerve was damaged beyond repair, leaving the finger dead and hooked. The dead, hooked finger would in future add more drama to the pointing gesture, when chastising one of the "little bleeders".

Syd was a little better at looking after bikes. He could oil them, it might have been with margarine, dripping or cod liver oil, but it would do. He could mend a puncture and pump up a tyre; that was about his limit. He enjoyed being out on a bike and would take one or two of the boys on long cycle journeys. He often lost his way, which led to unscheduled lengthening of the rides, meaning he brought one or two very tired and grumpy little boys home to Mary.

Syd encouraged and taught all the boys to ride bikes, and there were falls, cuts and grazes sustained by all of them, but Mick took the prize for the most spectacular crash. On the sudden realisation that he could remain upright on his two-wheeler bike while it was still in motion, he looked to the spectators for approval and promptly ran into the lamp-post at the corner of Oakhill Road. He received a very bad cut on his head and a quick dunking under the cold tap soon made him forget his pain and embarrassment.

Mick's encounter with the lamp-post was surprising, for every kid in the street knew where this particular lamp-post was as it was the source and focal point for most of the play activities in the street. It was a maypole, a wicket, a meeting point, a skipping rope and anchor. It acted as a giant hoopla for cycle tyres, it could be scuffed up or stones could be thrown breaking the glass.

As well as the street, the pieces of wasteground and the woods and fields close by were all playgrounds for the children of the street. Outside the corner shop was another assembling point for the children, particularly if a few empty lemonade bottles had been retrieved and some more pop or tizer was afforded by the few pennies received. A number of children would sit around the full pop bottle and watch the purchaser start to swig, hoping he would tire, full of gas, and pass the bottle around. They would watch him pick up small stones from the pavement and put them into the half empty pop, causing it to bubble furiously. They also hoped if the bottle was passed around, they wouldn't be the last to receive it and end up with a mouth full of stones.

It was on the step outside the corner shop that Brownie, a clever and crafty boy, decided to play a trick on two of the older boys. Brownie noticed a block of white washing soap by the mangle in the back yard of No. 37. He figured that it could be carved and made to look like a block of chocolate squares. He was right; his carving skills did make it look convincingly like chocolate.

He offered this to Bernie and Ivor, the older boys of the gang. Young Mick had been following and admiring the skills of his elder brother, and could hardly contain his excitement as he watched the pieces being put into their mouths. These were rough, tough lads that were receiving the soap, and you didn't mess with them without some escape route; Mick had been warned by Brownie to run like mad across the wasteground and up the back garden for home. They gained time as Bernie and Ivor were spitting out the frothy, soapy mass and made it safely inside the back door of No. 37.

Mary, cooking at the range in the back room, heard the loud and solid slam of the door and exclaimed, "You frightened the life out of me, and what have you two divils been up to now?" She soon found out when she saw the white soap shavings down by the mangle, and the boys got the crooked finger gesture and a clip about their ears.

CHAPTER
TEN

Boy Gangs

Over the years, many boy gangs were raised in Caenwood Road and the gangs gave the road a reputation that resulted in it being called "Do-as-you-like Street". The gangs fought with sticks and threw stones and crab apples at their enemies, the rival gangs from roads close by. Read Road and Taylor Road had their gangs, as did Kingston Road in Leatherhead. Oakhill Road and Oakhill Close, immediate neighbours to Caenwood Road, never formed viable gangs themselves as they were too close to the powerful "Do-as-you-like Street" gangs. Tough boys from these streets formed an alliance and joined forces with the Caenwood boys. Friends that formed the gangs spent a lot of time together as they were all about the same age. They walked to school together, spent all day at school and played in the evenings and weekends together.

Because of the age range, the Brown brothers would have been in three or four separate gangs from the street. Brownie and Mick would have been in the same gang with Ivor and Bernie, and no doubt after the soap incident, would have had to bribe or exercise their diplomatic skills to avoid a bashing. Many other boys would have been in their gang too, perhaps up to ten in all. The boys from the posh end of the road were seldom allowed to join the gangs, but there were a few exceptions. Pop Brant was one in Ivor and Bernie's gang.

The gang that Buster (Buttons) and Skinny (Bagpipes) were in was very creative and active, and contained many members from both the posh end of Caenwood Road and Oakhill Road. Their members included Biggy Lightfoot, Tingy and Stinker Stiles, and Fatty Wellings from Oakhill Road. There was Bonzo Bartholomew, Buster and Skinny Brown and Ginger Adams from the top end of Caenwood Road; Pecker Woodhouse, David Mercer and Prof. Symonds from the posh end of the road. Monkey Diggins, who lived on Barnett Wood Lane just at the top of Caenwood Road, was also a member of this gang.

One day a member of this gang spied some boys from the Kingston Road gang on their territory. This was not just any part of their territory; this was their sacred site, a veritable goldmine of a playground, the Dump.

The Dump had resulted from the backfilling of a large clay pit which had been dug for clay just before 1900. In area, it was about three acres, and by the 1940s had long been filled to overflowing with Victorian and Edwardian rubbish. This resulted in a landscape of small hills and hillocks covered with light scrub and grass, and on the edges where it joined fields, larger trees grew, including crab apple and sloe.

No finer place could be found for the amusement of the boys; there were lots of places to hide and ammunition provided with the crab apples, stones and pieces of pottery. There was treasure to dig up, there were snakes to taunt and catch with forked sticks, and in the winter the water trapped between the hillocks froze and made safe shallow skating areas. This territory had to be defended.

Incensed, the gang chased the invaders back across the railway line, the accepted territory boundary. The enemy had risked death crossing the railway lines when they invaded and now they risked it again on the retreat, this time bombarded with crab apples.

When the Kingston Road gang got to the other side of the line, and back on their own territory, they felt safe and decided to make a stand. The only ammunition they could find were stones from the fields and when it got this serious, the opposing side had to resort to similar tactics. The stone-throwing went on for ages and only halted when a train passed. A late delivery of a stone which struck a train must have resulted in the Police being called. Not really the Police, but the local Policeman for Ashtead, whose nickname was Podge.

Podge had propped his bike up against a rough field hedge on the Caenwood Road side of the field, and on entering the field, was quickly spotted by the warring gangs. They dispersed, the Caenwood boys making for the safe hiding places in the dump. Podge could be seen reading the Riot Act to the bushes, knowing that the gang members were in there somewhere. He would not leave until the act had been read, and the gang would not emerge until he departed.

This gang, as with all the street gangs before and after them, played all the games and got up to all the mischief that boy gangs do. They played football and cricket in the street and steered spokeless cycle wheels for hoops, skilfully knocking over the opponent's wheel without grounding their own. This was their Battle of Britain, they were the pilots and Bonzo was a very good pilot too.

Scrumping of apples, plums and pears was a favourite pastime, but not without its risks. The established orchards were in the bigger, older houses along Barnett Wood Lane towards Ashtead Station. The boys would tuck their sleeveless jumpers into their short trousers and tighten their belts a notch or two, giving them a useful carrying pouch for the spoils. The fruit was mainly windfalls, but the occasional stick or two was lobbed into the branches to down a ripened bunch. If Podge, the gardener or owners of the house were sighted, the boys would all bunk off as fast as they could, holding one hand across the top of their jumpers to prevent the fruit bouncing out.

On one scrumping expedition, Monkey Diggins, a tough athletic lad, ran off at such a rate, that the fruit not only bounced out of the top of the jumper but the jumper was released from the grip of the belt. His swag bounced along the lane and all but betrayed him as he ran to the sanctuary of his home on Barnett Wood Lane.

Another reason for the early release of the fruit would be if a wasp had been inadvertently placed in the pouch along with the fruit. When the sting was felt, there was a frantic war dance, a rapid release of the fruit and a vigorous slap about the body by yourself and your pals. This usually shifted the attacking wasp, but often resulted in the injured, pulsating insect falling deeper into your underwear.

Buster and Stinker were not averse to playing tricks or setting up other members of their own or other gangs. One dark evening, they set a large trap of loose sticks and brushwood in Green Lane for Biggy Lightfoot. On a regular time of an evening, he would cycle fast down the lane; he was a very keen cyclist and had a very good bike. An unmade track edged with trees and bushes, Green Lane was a continuation of Oakhill Road, running parallel with the railway line towards Ashtead Station.

Buster and Stinker crouched in the bushes and awaited the fun. The bumping of the tyres on the unmade track was heard, the small dim headlight was seen; they giggled, then hushed. Then crash, the bike hit the barrier, but instead of a youthful exclamation from Biggy, a deeper, grown-up male voice was heard delivering curses and swear words. They had caught an unexpectedly big fish and did not stay around to find out who it was, but faded into the darkness of the blackthorn bushes.

Green Lane seemed to be a favoured place for Buster and Stinker's pranks, for they carried out another crime in the lane. It was an alternative route to Barnett Wood Lane when the children returned from school, near the Oakhill Road end of the lane, and on the left was a small, lightly built cottage, partly hidden by the trees and bushes. The cottage was a place of mystery to small children; they would hurry past it, believing it to be the home of a witch. Noises were heard at the cottage, smoke left the chimney, but no one was ever seen.

On their way home from school one day, Buster and Stinker decided to solve some of the mystery of the cottage. Theirs was a simple strategy: lob stones on to the roof and see if anyone emerged. Their fear of the place wouldn't allow them to stick around long enough to find out, and they ran off after the first volley.

At school the next day, it was announced that a complaint had been received about the incident, and the culprits would be found among the children using the Green Lane route home. Two older boys, Prof. Symonds and Stinker's elder brother Tingy, were deemed to have been responsible and they took the cane across the hand from the Head, Miss McCartney, like the tough little soldiers they were. The scheming culprits kept mum, but never did find out who lived in the scary cottage.

The Adams family lived at No. 39 and were subjected to all the arguments, noise and comings and goings at No. 37. Mr Adams was convinced that any petty crime committed for miles around was planned and executed from No. 37. He may not have understood the control that the practice and teachings of the Catholic Church, including regular attendance, the confessional and the threat of eternal damnation, had on the Brown family. All this and two high principled parents, with the mother not averse to using corporal punishment, would be enough to keep the children on a reasonably straight path.

Ginger Adams had joined the Boys' Brigade and most of the gang to which he belonged had joined the Scouts, including his contemporary gang neighbours, Buster and Flint (Skinny). Although Ginger had become estranged from the group, he did become a hero when he volunteered to negotiate for the release of a hostage taken when the gang had been going on an expedition to the Dump.

The hostage was not very important to the gang, not even a member, but an annoying liability in the shape of Buster and Flint's younger brother Fred, or Alec as he was always called. Mary did not like losing any of her children and if you were the elder, you were responsible; Buster feared her temper.

Ginger must have volunteered before he knew that the hostage had been taken by Dixie, the gypsy. Dixie lived in a caravan sited on the Barnett Wood Lane side of the Dump, and acted as caretaker for the farmer, preventing damage to fences, corn and haystacks caused by the local children. An earlier gang had set alight a haystack while playing with matches, and also, although it wasn't caused by any gang, one of Dixie's caravans had burnt down.

The gypsy liked to be left in peace and kept dogs and a pony about his caravan as a deterrent for small children. Buster had once received a light kick in the head from the pony, so there was much reluctance to go near the gypsy site on the way to the Dump. For this reason, the gang, with hangers-on in tow, gave Dixie a wide berth and had made it to the dump without being seen by him.

Children's games, though, may start quietly, but they quickly reach a level of noise to wake the dead, let alone a sleeping gypsy. Dixie easily crept near to the noisy group and pounced upon them as a fox would on a bunch of frolicking rabbits, and seized the most vulnerable: young Alec. The others scattered and returned to regroup near the hedge at the back of No. 37. Ginger, the volunteer rescuer, couldn't back down and looked suitably authoritative in his Boys' Brigade uniform with a pill box hat, broad white sash and leather belt. He marched across the field, negotiated with the gypsy and returned with Alec, the bewildered little liability.

CHAPTER
ELEVEN

Life's Dangers

When children run free to play, they always encounter danger and risk injury, death or molestation by men, and the family were not immune to these dangers. The war brought the bombing and its aftermath, the debris that tempted young children and the increased traffic due to troop movements. The children themselves risked their lives when crossing the railway line, and played in or near rivers and water-filled clay pits. They learned to run from the seedy men offering them sweets from a grimy paper bag or the dirty mac-clad flashers they encountered.

Even on trips when Syd and Mary were present, the dangers lurked and they remained vigilant. When Syd took his tribe to the pictures, many friends would tag along and make up a group of about a dozen. When they sat down in the cinema in one line, it was seldom long before a predatory male would park himself at the opposite end of the group to Syd. On these occasions, Syd was on his guard, and with a quiet word would send the man away.

On a picnic trip to the River Mole, young Alec, ever the one for getting into danger, toddled into the water and sank down into the weeds. Flint, the elder brother responsible at the time, quickly sensed the danger and pulled him out.

Oxshott Heath was a four-mile walk from Caenwood Road, but was worth the trip for the excitement of tunnelling into sandy cliffs that edged the basin-shaped disused sand pit. Buster and Flint were buried when a mass of sand and soil collapsed on them. The party were aware that Buster had been digging out in one cave and he was hurriedly pulled out, but it was some time before it was noticed that Flint was missing. There was a lot of bawling, shouting and frantic digging before Flint was uncovered and pulled out by his hair.

The neighbours in the street were extremely tolerant, philosophical ("Boys will be boys") or outright hostile towards the boy gangs. Ted and Daisy Steer were the tolerant sort, and this was just as well for their house was on the corner of Oakhill Road, opposite No. 37 and next to the lamp-post; the hub of all the childish and youthful activity in the street. Their corner house was enclosed by a long run of close-boarded fencing. This type of fence was good for chalking on stumps, goalposts or targets, and so Ted and Daisy were regularly subjected to the thump of balls and other missiles against their fence.

Ted was a keen participant in the "Dig For Victory" campaign during the war and grew vegetables in his back and front gardens, which took regular poundings from the balls and missiles that crossed the fence. However, he wisely situated his greenhouse at the far end of his back garden, which ended further down

Caenwood Road near the posh houses. Ted would patiently tend to the damaged plants, dig over the tiny footprints in the soil, and with hammer and nail would fix back the loosened boards to his fence. Because of their tolerance, Ted and Daisy were not subjected to other annoying pranks and games that children enjoy; these were reserved for the most aggressive and least sympathetic of the neighbours.

One such prank was a game called "Knock Down Ginger", and it was not knocking over our neighbour, Ginger Adams. On the dark autumn and winter evenings, a small group of kids would creep up to a front door, bang the knocker hard, then run and hide. This might be repeated if the person opening the door thought the knock imagined, or caused by the wind. The purpose was to annoy, to get chased or an act of revenge, a test of courage and endurance and to practice concealment skills.

When the war ended and fireworks and bonfires were allowed again, November the 5th became a major event in the street. All the burnable rubbish was trawled and stacked higher and higher, and it was a source of pride for a street gang to have the biggest fire around. If a rival gang's fire was bigger, a raid might be mounted to burn it down before the due date. A bonfire built on the grass roundabout in Oakhill Close was burned down prematurely one year, and no one admitted responsibility, but a guard was mounted on the one in Caenwood Road.

The wasteground between No. 35 where Ted and Phil Cullen lived, and the corner shop, was the site of

November 5th bonfires after the war, but when this land was built on in 1948, the fires were raised on the grassed area at the top of the street on the left. This strip of land was quite narrow and next to a close-boarded fence of the house sited in Barnett Wood Lane.

By this time the street had something of a reputation to maintain with regard to their bonfires, and dads and grandads had an enthusiastic input into building them. The helpers heaped the rubbish higher and higher around a driven anchor post in the centre. They persuaded Bert Hagerman, who had a very big workshop on the right at the top of the road, to part with a pile of old cycle tyres to add to the pyre. The man whose garden fence was close to the fire was concerned as he watched the heap grow, but was powerless in the face of such frenzied community activity.

When the fire was lit and crackled and roared, the flames rising high, smoke appeared to be rising from the close-boarded fence. The house-owner cracked, seized his opportunity and phoned the fire brigade. The excitement was mounting on hearing the clanging, approaching fire engine racing up to Barnett Wood Lane from Leatherhead. The firemen were very calm about the incident, reluctant to spoil the evening for so many people. They examined the fence, decided it was not smoke but steam rising, hosed it down and drove off with a final clang. This left one angry householder, but a happy, cheering crowd.

Fireworks were hard to get at the time, and rumours of supplies arriving at local shops would cause queues to form outside the shops within hours of the news spreading. The shopkeepers were often very fair with their selling and only allowed so many per person to prevent greedy people profiteering. They'd had the war years, when lots of items were rationed and most things in short supply, to work out their fair distribution policy.

The bangers and squibs were the favourite fireworks of the boys. They'd light them and throw them into porches, causing echoing blasts, or secretly drop them behind each other or girls. They placed them in rabbit holes or hollow trees, thrilled at all the explosive results. The youths that had joined the Army and were on leave often bought thunderflashes home with them. Thunderflashes were large bangers used to add explosive realism for soldiers in training, and were not meant to be found at civilian celebrations.

There was a practice with boys that if a smouldering firework was thrown at you, you could pick it up and lob it on before it exploded. It was fair, it was also risky and Biz (Paddy) was unlucky enough to have a banger explode as he bent to pick it up. The blast stunned him and disorientated, he ran around in circles, claiming he was "death in one ear". He may well have pronounced "deaf" as "death" before the event, but if he'd grabbed a thunderflash, it might well have caused his death.

CHAPTER
TWELVE

Spy in our Midst

The end of the war brought much relief and celebration to the street, and both ends came together for at least two street parties. The lower end of the street had a number of artisans living there, and they fixed up a stage with electric lighting and loudspeakers. The street was a cul-de-sac and the whole lower end was decked out in balloons, bunting and flags criss-crossing the road. Trestle tables and chairs were lined down the middle and the ladies placed coloured paper as tablecloths to cover them. They then lined out the plates and cutlery, followed by a homemade assortment of sandwiches and many types of cakes and coloured jellies. There was a fancy dress parade for the children with an opportunity to perform a party-piece on the stage, and for the grown-ups the dancing would go on long into the night. The music came from a gramophone or piano placed to the side of the stage.

Mary and Syd put a lot of effort into providing the children with fancy dress. Thelma was dressed as a boy scout. Biz and Scrapper (Alec) were cowboys, and Buster and Flint straw-boatered song and dance men, complete with canes. Brownie and Mick, into their teens by now, preferred not to be embarrassed by any dressing up.

The song and dance men were well rehearsed by Syd for their soft shoe shuffle and song, which they would perform on stage. The performance went down well with all but their friends, who giggled and poked fun at them. Gaynor Gadd, a chubby little girl from the posh end of the street, was dressed as the singing film star Carmen Miranda, and while singing her song "Tic'o Tic'o Tock", she wobbled her porky little body and braved the sniggering boys.

The Medwin girls, Cynthia and Diana, both very posh girls from the posh end of the street, were dressed as a gypsy and a ballet dancer. Diana, the ballet dancer, did her party piece but forgot her steps and withdrew from the stage in tears, her wrist to her forehead in classic dramatic style, exclaiming "I can't go on!" All the adults were sympathetic, the lads less so, there were many more exciting things to do; they were only there for the soft drinks, sandwiches, jellies and cakes. Buster felt her hurt though, for Diana was his first secret love, and he would sort the sniggering boys out with a bashing later.

Syd had aspirations to present his own Brown boys choir at the show, but his control over the group at rehearsals was not sufficient to produce a credible sound. Discipline would collapse in fits of uncontrollable laughter from the moment he was mimicked, by various subversives in the choir, as he tried several attempts to pitch the key best suited for the young choristers.

Syd took his singing quite seriously and sang tenor with the Ashtead Choral Society, and from the time he went to work at the Ex-Services Welfare Society, he had had free singing lessons from a professional singing coach in London. His expenses were paid by the Welfare Society, who along with many other welfare groups set up after the First World War, believed that music, particularly singing, had much therapeutic value with the men whose nerves had been shattered by war experiences.

He was not, though, a very inspirational choirmaster, and it was Mary that had more success at getting the boys to work together with her emotional rebel-rousing Irish songs. The boys had been much younger then, and had not developed too far towards the strongly independent characters they would become.

Although Diana's dramatic withdrawal at the street party was caused by a memory lapse, her father had every reason to expect a sabotage attempt on the proceedings. Some weeks before, Mr Medwin had been sprayed with water from the front bedroom window of No. 37 when he was striding past on his way home from work. Mr Medwin was a very purposeful, upright and smartly dressed man, he wore coloured bow ties and walked with his shoulders back like a marching soldier. The little perpetrators of this incident were the youngest boys, Scrapper and Biz (Paddy). They had made water projectors from old cycle inner-tubes from Mr Hagerman's workshop and were trying them out.

Mr Medwin did stand for a while remonstrating, but as he got wetter he decided to retreat and marched off.

Another weapon invented by Scrapper and Biz for use from the bedroom window was the super pea shooter — although it wasn't for shooting peas, it was for firing ball-bearings, and these too were collected from Hagerman's workshop. The blowpipe used was the aluminium rail supporting the curtains at the window of the bedroom. This was just the right size and when Scrapper took it down, and drew the curtains off to test it, he sucked in at first and swallowed the spider that had made its home inside the pipe.

After coughing up the mucus-encased spider, Scrapper filled his lungs with air, put a few ball-bearings in his mouth, aimed the super gun at a house 75 yards away and fired. The boys had no doubt that their missiles had reached the target and gladly added the new weapon to their armoury for future mischievous and dangerous pranks, confident that the gun could not be traced. The gun was never found, innocently disguised as a curtain rail.

At the top of the street on the right was a small area of ancient oak trees, which was probably the remains of Caen Wood. This was another favourite play area and known by the children as the Toppy, it being at the top of the street. Most of the trees were too hard to climb, not having any low branches for small children to make a start. But one large, gnarled, old tree was climbable and hollow. This tree was the place to run to and hide if you had angered Mum enough to deserve a good whack. Mary was no runner or climber, and by the time she reached the oak, out of breath, the young offender would be hidden deep out of sight in the hollow. By the time she was ready to talk the boy down, her temper had cooled, and a good telling off became the punishment.

Bert Hagerman's workshop and garages for his cars were very near the hollow oak, and he must have seen Mrs Brown at times, the woman from down the road with all the kids, apparently talking to the oak tree, but he said nothing.

It was believed by all the lads in the street that Bert was a German spy and, for this reason, they tested his patience by freely entering his workshop to take away the many items they needed for their pranks and games. They believed he could not risk breaking his cover by cuffing a boy's ear if he thought the lad was walking off with too much loot. Most of the stuff the boys took was scrap material: the punctured cycle inner-tubes, the spokeless wheels and the shiny ball-bearings which were collected from the earthen floor. The workshop was an Aladdin's Cave for small boys and fired their inventive imaginations.

Bert and his family were a mystery. He lived in the Edwardian house with two old ladies who were seldom seen, except peeping from behind a curtain at the window or through a part-opened door when someone called at the house. He spoke in a thick, foreign accent, mostly mumbling his words, making him hard to understand. He was old, small and nervy, fidgeting about his yard and workshop mumbling to himself. He wore dirty, old clothes and a flat cap when in his workshop, but if he hired out one of his grand cars as a taxi, he donned a crumpled dark suit and shiny-peaked chauffeur's hat.

Bert made a little money by mending or making up bikes for sale. His bikes were nothing special, but if a lad was lucky enough for his parents to afford one, it was certain to be in maroon, the only colour Bert had in his workshop. His other source of income was his taxi service. His two grand taxi cars were kept locked in the rickety, wooden garages around his yard. When Bert wasn't about, the boys would look through cracks in the garage doors and marvel at the well-polished machines. Bert treasured his cars and when there were no children around he'd bring them from the garages into the yard, and lovingly wash and polish them.

Every boy would have loved to ride in one of the cars, but had little hope as taxi rides cost money. Scrapper and Biz, well known to Bert, did get to ride in the car more than once. Tessie, Mary's larger-than-life friend from No. 43, used Bert's taxis for pub visits. By this time, her son Peter was about five years old and rather than leave her son to the rough and tumble of the street, she took some of the rough from the street as minders for the boy. Scrapper and Biz got to ride in Bert's taxis and thought it grand, much better than the smelly buses.

The trips weren't meant to be long, just to pick up a bottle or two of stout for home consumption, but they were seldom short. The first stop had to be Percy Fair's sweet shop to buy some sweets for the boys. Once there must have been an argument in the shop, perhaps over payment for the jelly babies, as Tessie came out backwards as though pushed. She fell on her backside on the pavement, picked herself up, adjusted the alignment of the fag in her mouth, brushed herself down and got back into the taxi, filling it with smoke and anger.

For some reason, the trips did not include visits to local pubs and The Victoria in Oxshott village about four miles away, was a particular favourite for Tessie. Perhaps they kept her preferred tipple, for when it was visited Tessie just had to have a quick one while she was there.

Children were not allowed in the bars in pubs, so the boys waited outside and eagerly expected, and in time received, the lemonade and Smith's crisps passed through the part opened doors. They also heard the excited din and smelled the thick smoky atmosphere that wafted past as the doors opened and closed, when the men staggered out to visit the outside lavatory. Bert sat in his car parked across the road and mumbled to himself.

Scrapper and Biz were in the same gang and among their members were the twins John and Dave Wellings from Oakhill Road, Georgy Cutter and Biff Bartholomew from Caenwood Road, and John and Pinhead Pete Edwards from Barnett Wood Lane. Scrapper had fought to gain his position as gang leader. He was regularly to be found locked in a sweaty challenge with another contender for the title, and for this reason received his nickname.

Scrapper led his little group on many expeditions and adventures, and although the Dump remained a favourite play area, the copse down Barnett Wood Lane was particularly enjoyed by this gang. They found in abundance the hazel needed for their bows and arrows, spending hours whittling the arrows to improve their accuracy and distance in flight, and the point to improve the penetration. The springy bows came from the older wood and the arrows from the fresh, straight, one-year old wood.

The coppice was regularly worked by Mr Ranger, a short, very old, bow-legged man who smoked a pipe, wore thick leather spats and looked not unlike Popeye facially. The gang would often know where Mr Ranger was working in the woods, and as a manoeuvre, would creep up to disturb his tranquillity with shouts and whoops, and he in turn feigned fright. Mr Ranger was part of the wood and his attuned senses would have informed him in good time of the approach of the boys; he was patient and tolerant of them.

The gang also liked to explore other play areas and walked for miles just to visit different places, and at times would encounter other small gangs of boys, who'd staunchly defend those areas known as their territory. Roundabouts then were large and always planted up with shrubs and trees. These proved to be good short stay game areas when the boys were passing by on some large adventure. The roundabout at the Plough was one such site, and was closely covered with shrubs in which to hide or to push an unwary friend. The boys might occasionally drop out, or be pushed into the surrounding road, but no gang member was ever lost this way as the traffic was so infrequent.

The roundabout on the Epsom Road, where the Leatherhead Bypass met it, was a short stay games area when the gang were on their way to the Fortyfoot Road Recreation Ground. The Fortyfoot Rec. was always kept in pristine condition, the flower borders tended, the grass and hedges neatly cut and trimmed, with no vandalised play equipment or litter left around, and it was seldom used. This deserted park was at the end of an unmade road, which contained a few very large houses with spacious gardens, but was lost on the abandonment of a grand scheme to develop an idyllic housing estate, complete with park and gardens. Scrapper liked to lead his little gang to the quiet, unspoilt places and was told by Syd of another such park across Ashtead Woods towards Epsom, on the Chessington side of town.

Syd offered to take the gang there one Saturday afternoon, and the troop duly assembled and set off. On reaching the Epsom to Chessington road, a short way out of Epsom, the group stopped to cross as it was busy, being market day. There was a commotion further down towards the town: a horse had bolted, pulling a cart full of unsold peaches from the market. The animal pulling the swaying cart sped by, littering the road with bruised, tumbling peaches, a feast for small boys.

They collected many and ate many, and continued their journey to discover the other lost park. Biff was the first lad whose bowels objected to the over-ripe, bruised, unsold peaches and left his mark on the slide, causing it to be abandoned for the rest of the trip. It was lucky for the boys that a large part of the journey home was through woods, with lots of cover to maintain their dignity, but they soon released their jumpers from their tight belts to discard any uneaten fruit.

A game the lads played in the twilight of autumn evenings was one that Scrapper had invented, and they called it "doll dolls on the lawn". The object was to gain access to the back gardens of the very large houses along Barnett Wood Lane, and there push one another into the beds and borders, and frolic until spotted by an irate householder, who might give chase. The lad that found himself entangled in the shrubbery would be at a disadvantage and need all his guile to escape.

The two Edwards boys, who were part of the gang, lived in one of the big houses in Barnett Wood Lane and so, with certain tolerated legitimacy, the gang could play in their garden in the full daylight hours. This was not to the liking of their grumpy grandfather who lived with them. The old man did not like his peace being disturbed and regularly chased the boys from the garden. He had reason enough when a carefully crafted arrow from a hazel bow passed through a pane of glass of the windbreak behind which he was dozing.

Grandad, in truth, was a belt and braces man. He mostly wore striped collarless shirts and baggy trousers with both braces and wide leather belt. The braces were for holding up the trousers and the belt for clouting unruly kids. Woken by the shattering event, Grandpa toddled down the path, believing he was moving at some speed towards the boys, a real Victorian disciplinarian, anger showing in his watery eyes.

Scrapper often had to display some brave act in leadership to impress his little comrades. He took a stand of teasing bravado and struck a boxer's pose to face the old man shaking down the path. Grandad stopped and reached for the buckle on his belt, but before it was released all the boys were across the road and into the Toppy and safety.

CHAPTER
THIRTEEN

Leaving Home

Scrapper, as his name might suggest and his antics might confirm, was an inventive and mischievous child, which may have been the reason he was left out on many outings with Mary. On the trips to London or holiday visits to John and Rose in Ireland, Mary felt she could only cope with two of the children at a time. The pairings were: Brownie and Mick, Buster and Flint, and Biz and Thelma. Scrapper and Syd were the only family members not to visit Ireland.

It was fun at home with Syd, and together with others left behind, they shared an erratic diet and much teasing and argument. Syd did some cooking and so did the boys, nothing very fancy though, and this was not expected as the family had survived on the Spartan diet of the war years. The favourites were fried bread, eggs, bacon, chips and custard for a sweet.

Syd overdid the cloves used to flavour the custard and as the boys never liked them, they would scoop them out before spooning the sweet liquid into their mouths. Buster and Flint were tired of fishing out the evil tasting cloves, and Flint flicked one forcefully from his bowl across the table. It landed on Syd's collar and stuck there with a blob of yellow custard. Syd had been sitting opposite, in deep concentration and thought over a newspaper he was reading, unaware of the sticky badge hanging on his collar. The boys sniggered at their secret, and quietly elected that Syd was a member of the yellow team.

Syd brought home from work, not the pheasants or pigeons to cook, but cut up steamed currant pudding. The pudding was the leftovers from the work's canteen, which was at the electric blanket factory owned by the Ex-Services Welfare Society. The pudding had been cut into thick round portions, and when Syd drew them from his greatcoat pockets, he'd brush or blow away the dust, debris and remains of his boiler fuel-collecting days, and offer it to the boys. When cleaned up, the pudding wasn't bad, and inspired many recipes including frying, grilling, toasting or with custard, butter or syrup.

Either the family tired of the pudding or supplies ran short, for Syd decided to purchase a canned steam pudding from the shop. It was a rhubarb steam pudding. The tin in which the pudding came was meant to be punctured before it was heated in the boiling water. Syd failed to do this, and when the can opener pierced the hot tin, the contents spluttered out like the bullets from a machine gun. Syd held the can in a teacloth at arms length, and turned around in confusion looking for a safe spot in which to place the hissing, spitting pudding. The panicked effort sprayed the walls with stringy rhubarb and pudding, with Michael Collins in the picture receiving his share. It was all cleared up before Mary and her youngest children returned from Ireland.

Caenwood Road always seemed alive with the comings and goings of the folk who lived there, and with the noise of the children, as well as chatting ladies by the shop or outside Granny Osborne's house. Even in the snow and ice of winter, when snowballs flew, and cold and busy gloved and ungloved hands patted snowmen into shape, the parents and grandparents would gather, shiver and talk about the weather. The children compacted snow to make a slide, and as it became more slippery, it grew longer and more dangerous until salted by a concerned adult. One such winter was so cold that a cooled, stone hot water bottle placed outside the bed by one of the Brown boys froze solid and cracked.

In the heat of spring and summer, the street was abuzz with the usual activities, and the chimes of the ice-cream van were added to this, a teasing sound if they couldn't afford or were denied one. The children without ice-creams would spread the rumour that the treat would cause an infection or typhoid, and intimidated the children lucky enough to have one.

At times a pack of dogs would roam the streets, chasing a bitch in season, and if a householder had the shame and taint of copulating animals outside their house, they'd throw a bucket of cold water over them. This practice was mostly carried out by old ladies.

The breadman came everyday except Sundays and Buster earned some money by helping Alan, the breadman. Buster became adept at retrieving the crusty loaves from the back of the van, using the long pole with the six inch nail in the end which pierced the bread. He would drag them back across the crumb-strewn floor of the van, and smiling, deliver them to householders.

The milk was delivered by Mr Cutter, Georgie's father, who lived at the top of Caenwood Road. He worked for the United Dairies, at the time delivering the bottled milk from horse and car-tyred carts. Mr Cutter employed the help of Biz and Scrapper on Saturdays, his busy day, when he collected the money.

The two boys enjoyed the rides on the cart; they sat high up in front with Mr Cutter, fascinated by the flapping reins, the smell of the horse and its enormous, shifting backside. But they retreated back along the walking platforms set either side of the cart above the wheels, in a fit of giggles if the horse farted or dropped its dung. The steaming dung did not remain long in the road before a householder appeared with a shovel and bucket, and retrieved it for the rhubarb growing in the back garden.

When the children reached 10 or 11, they all found jobs bringing in a little money which was passed over to Mary to help with the family finances. Helping the breadman and the milkman would have only brought in pennies, as Alan the breadman and Mr Cutter the milkman were working men trying to raise their own families. They tolerated the smiling, giggling little helpers and felt in some small way they were helping a large, struggling family.

The job most often obtained by the children was the morning paper-round. A round might bring in the princely sum of 5 shillings or 7 shillings per week, with extra if one did a Sunday round. The job was pleasant enough on warm, bright spring and summer mornings, but come the sleet, fog, ice and snow of autumn and winter and the dark early mornings, the job became almost unbearable.

The incentive to struggle on to at least beyond Christmas was the promise that a huge bonus would be gathered from the customers: the Xmas box. The Xmas box often amounted to the equivalent of a month's wages, but depended on the boy delivering the papers on time, dry, unscrunched, not dog chewed, the gate closed, and on the generosity of the customer.

The four eldest boys bravely held on to paper-round jobs for varying periods, but the two youngest, Scrapper and Biz, preferred gardening. They'd both spent a lot of time with Syd when he did his gardening for the people living in the large houses in the lanes, and had picked up some knowledge and skill. When they were 10 or 11, they found their own gardening work and would spend hours on their knees hand-weeding a path or border for sixpence per hour. With their record of mischief, this was probably all they were worth, and they were fortunate to have some very kind customers, among them a nurseryman, a retired naval captain, a head gardener and a businessman.

Mick was the first to leave home. He joined the navy when he was fifteen, which meant that a spare bed was available in the front bedroom, the "barrack room".

However, the chance for extra space was short lived for it wasn't long before Mick was bringing home navy pals for weekend leave. His pals probably lived too far from their training ship to make it worth their while going to their own homes, and certainly the cramped conditions at No. 37 would have given the sailors the qualifications and experience for serving on a submarine.

The habit of bringing pals home was established over the next few years when Brownie, Buster, Flint and Biz joined the Army as their call up came. Scrapper had failed his Army medical and was therefore not responsible for turning the front bedroom into an actual barrack room for many weekends during the 1950s.

The boys were all generous towards the family, and the ones that were serving in the forces all sent back money to Mary to help out. The younger ones, left at home, also put into the communal fund part of their meagre earnings, and by this time Mary must have been thinking that her major worries were over. She was in her early fifties, had been totally grey-haired since she was thirty-five, and had worked, worried and struggled for almost twenty-five years to bring up her family. She had reason to believe her life's work done.

Syd had helped where he could, but because of his depressed periods, he could never sustain lasting support. Mary had once encouraged him to leave the low-paid job with the charity, but the labouring job he took on with the council only lasted a few days before he returned one day in tears. He needed the stress-free, secure job with the charity. They understood, and took him back.

About this period, Syd suffered his worst bouts of depression and on at least two occasions spent a few weeks in Nethern, a mental institution near Croydon in Surrey. Nethern was an ornate, red-brick Victorian-built madhouse set in acres of parkland and gardens in which there were a few houses and many ancillary buildings. The main building was vast, with a maze of long, cold corridors and side rooms, which echoed with strange sounds. The grounds and corridors were always busy with confused, dazed, shuffling people and purposeful men in white coats. It was here Syd received painful electric shock treatment, and he believed it improved his condition, but sadly there was no lasting cure.

Mary would take the long bus ride to visit him when she could, but there were bus changes to negotiate which made it a difficult journey. She often took one or two of the younger children with her, which must have been a very worrying and confusing experience for them. Mental illness was a secret not openly talked about then; it was a stigma suffered within the family.

Syd must have wondered when life's burdens would be lifted from him, and during his low moments would pace the house repeating to himself, "Oh dear! What a bloody life." These events didn't inspire any of the children confidently to enter adulthood where it appeared things were very tough.

Mary would counter his negative attitude and foster her philosophy of "Live life today, and to the full". This she did, and with extra money to hand, she visited the pub more often, which meant she often got drunk. This state may have given her much needed relief, but on occasions it caused embarrassment to her adolescent younger children. Once she staggered onto the bus home, and came across Paddy (Biz) and a group of friends returning from an evening out. She caused further embarrassment to Paddy by fawning over him, and in a fit of nostalgia and slurred words, declared to the company that he was her little baby, her last son.

On another occasion, she had cycled to the pub on one of the bikes that had been maintained by Syd; light-headed, she had peddled and wobbled on her return. Just before she reached the Toppy, where the children were playing, she fell off the bike and badly cut her face and hands. Thelma, playing with friends, ran to pick up her mother, and the little group of ten-year olds helped Mary to her feet and escorted her home to dress her wounds and put her to bed.

The push up the stairs required the assistance of Thelma's elder brothers, but with work commitments and their Army call up, the beefy older boys were not available. Scrapper and Biz would have to suffice; the trio embarked on the task to push and pull the near dead weight of their weepy, sentimental, dazed mother up the stairs to bed. All the while, Mary was claiming she'd only had a pint of Guinness and was not drunk.

Thelma was sympathetic and concerned. Biz could work out his anger for the embarrassment he felt, and Fred, ever the one to see humour in a situation, would mimic two workmen trying to shift a heavy load in difficult circumstances with "Up your end a bit, 'Arry" or "Down your end a bit, Bert". At least it was better than Mary breaking out with "Danny Boy"; she could never sing very well, even when sober.

Her trips to the pub meant she met some desperate and needy people, and one religious fanatic and down-and-out was invited to live in the house. He occupied the box bedroom where Syd had moved to when Thelma was born, which meant Syd moved back to the middle bedroom with Thelma and her mother.

This arrangement did not last long, and the man left after a few days, but not before Scrapper and Biz had witnessed one of his bizarre habits. They'd looked in on him in the box room and found him bouncing on the bed, balancing on the sagging mattress, his arms outstretched, and looking to the heavens. In each hand he held an orange, and he was singing "Jesus Wants Me for a Sunbeam". This scene was too weird even for the boys, who had seen some odd practices both at home and at church, and they attempted to withdraw. But the man had seen them, and he simply stopped his singing and bouncing, and threw them an orange each saying, "Here you are, here's a horringe for you."

As the money worries eased, other worries came to the fore and about this time there were many. As well as Syd's periods of hospitalisation, young Fred (Scrapper) was sent to hospital to have two abscesses removed from his groin. After the surgery at Epsom hospital, he was sent to Cuddington Isolation Hospital in the hope that the wounds might heal before the boisterous youngster was freely roaming the woods and fields again. During the long weeks at Cuddington, Fred had regular visits from his mother, although it was an awkward journey for her. The reassurance from his mother was necessary, even for a tough little twelve year old like Scrapper, for at the hospital a number of people were recovering from polio, some encased in the dreaded iron lungs.

Paddy was also taken to hospital, for the removal of his appendix, within a year or two of his father and brother. This stay was short, but might have been longer if Scrapper had not stopped making him laugh, stitch-splitting laughter, about the antics at home while he was away.

Mary's health was failing too. As well as her persistent chesty "cawf", a large fatty lump appeared on her left shoulder. It was thought to be cancerous, and she was taken to hospital for its removal. It proved to be benign, but the surgeon was worried about Mary's general health, and decided she needed a prolonged period of rest. He arranged for her to enter a convalescent hospital south of Guildford, where she enjoyed the restorative daily Guinness that they supplied, returning to No. 37 a little fitter for the fight.

Both Mary and Syd smoked, but finances did not allow them to follow the habit to excess and, as with the drink, a little seemed to go a long way. Mary's "cawf" was with her all her adult life, the spirits she occasionally knocked back were "Just for me cawf". Syd rolled his own cigarettes and was so mean with tobacco that half the fag paper would go up in flames and burn the hairs inside his nose before it smouldered the meat of the cigarette. He didn't smoke much but the hairs in his nose got a roasting when he did.

Mary was very anxious that the children, particularly the boys, would not "catch" their father's depression and eccentricities, constantly reminding them to act or behave in a certain way, or they would turn out like their father. The words she spoke had a powerful effect on boys reaching puberty, and implied that the man who had encouraged them to walk, swim, ride, box and sing, and to appreciate the joys of gardening, was somehow seriously deficient. Mary spoke in innocence, but her words caused confusion in the boys' minds. She also wasted those words, for whether she liked it or not, there was a part of Syd in all her children.

Syd was a quiet, thoughtful, humorous, eccentric man, who on occasions was burdened with severe bouts of debilitating depression. His eccentricities were nearly always the source of amusement, and his opinions were often paradoxical, leaving one with the thought that he might be pulling your leg. He did not give fatherly advice to the boys about sex, and when he was teasingly pressed on the subject by one of the boys, he replied "I'm not interested in sex, son, never have been."

When he tried to talk to his two youngest sons about the arrangements when he died, i.e. "Look after your mother" and so on, he could not bring himself to say the words "When I die, son . . . " but would say "When I go, son . . . " The boys knowing full well what he meant would in turn ask him "Where are you going, Dad?" His reply would be "Now, be serious, you know what I mean." Of course, it never really could be serious with him.

On cold days he wore an old Army greatcoat, and with his trilby hat pulled low over his eyes, and hands thrust deep into his pockets, he would trudge the mile to work each day. He might stop to talk to a dog or cat, a known person or stranger; it would depend on his mood. If his mood was quiet and pensive, or it was the weekend with the house full of noisy, youthful soldiers, sailors or civvies playing cards, he would depart unnoticed on a long, lonely walk, drifting for miles. His vagrant appearance would attract the attention of the police who, after questioning him, would bring him back home to confirm his identity. They would have understood his need to escape when they witnessed the noisy, smoky, speakeasy atmosphere in the backroom of No. 37 Caenwood Road.

There was a little more space left at the house when Mick left for the Navy and Brownie went to do his National Service, apart from weekends that is. Brownie became Geoff or Geoffrey, as he joined the Royal Horse Artillery, where he became a sergeant, and Brownie sounded as though he might have been a Second World War Spitfire pilot. Buster and Flint had both been to the Grammar School in Epsom, and so great things were expected of them. Buster left to take a job at Epsom library, which was appropriate because he liked reading, and from then on was always called William or Bill. Flint left school a year or two later and worked for a firm of accountants with the idea that he might become qualified one day. He soldiered on, as

Stan or Stanley, with computing the endless columns of figures until his Army call-up came. He joined the Royal Electrical and Mechanical Engineers. Where he was offered, but turned down, the chance to train as an officer.

While working at the library, Bill had befriended a carpenter who had been working there on some maintenance. The lad was a year or two older than Bill and enjoyed his visits to No. 37, where it seemed to him it was all happening with lots of youthful, friendly banter and argument. He would visit any time he was working in the area, and one day he visited when Mary and Stan were home, which was fortunate in view of what happened.

The three of them were sitting around the table in the back room enjoying a cup of tea and chatting quite normally. The cosied teapot, as always, stood on the table with used cups, plates, knives and forks dotted around. The mood of the visitor became agitated as he searched for words to clarify a point he wished to make in conversation, his voice raised in frustration. His face flushed, his eyes bulged, and he would not respond to any quiet reasoning by Mary or Stan. He picked up the teapot and crashed it to the floor; this was followed by the cups, one by one. Then the teacloth was snatched away, clearing the tabletop. The demented youth then decided to pick items from the floor to smash against the walls.

Mary and Stan were terrified. There was no way of calming or restraining this strong, bulky youth, so they retreated to the scullery and closed the door. An ambulance was called and the lad, who was manageable by then, was quietly led away and taken to Nethern Mental Hospital. He had had a nervous breakdown.

This same youth had introduced his elder brother to the household and he often visited evenings after his work. Mary and Syd were not wary enough of this man when he requested to say goodnight to Paddy and Fred in their beds. The packed front bedroom meant Paddy and Fred still had to sleep in the same bed. The man entered the room, chatted for a while and gradually eased his hand under the bedclothes and fondled each lad in turn around the genitals.

They both instinctively knew this was not right, and shuffled and turned away from the groping hand. The man asked, "Do you like that?" and they both replied "No." He replied "Oh, you don't like Ursula." Next morning the boys reported the incident to Mary and the man was told never to visit the house again. Mary wisely chose not to tell his strong, volatile brother of the incident, for she believed he would have killed him.

As a sergeant in the smart Royal Horse Artillery, Geoffrey was attractive to the girls, and there was one in particular, Ursula, he was attracted to. Ursula was a beautiful, blonde, Scandinavian au pair who worked for Dr Mellon for whom Mary did regular cleaning at his surgery. Geoffrey and Ursula had a fling and it must have got a bit out of hand as Geoffrey was recalled from Germany, where he was stationed and came home to sort things out.

They were sorted out; Mary promised Dr Mellon she would keep her randy sons away from his staff, and

Geoffrey learned that playing Doctors and Nurses for real was an expensive exercise. A collection by Mary to pay Geoffrey's fare back to Germany was made, and Paddy was persuaded by Mary to part with his 30 shillings gardening money he had saved from many hours weeding.

CHAPTER
FOURTEEN

The End is Near

Mick, having joined the Navy as a lad of fifteen, had said that he'd wanted space (didn't they all?) and a chance to see the world. He got the space, saw some of the world, but did not like the discipline. Mary tried to get him released from his commitment to the Navy by citing the fact that he regularly wet the bed. He had, of course, been doing this for years at home, and that is why he always had a bed to himself. The appeals failed and Mick spent many years sailing around the world and would admit that the sailor's uniform added much to his charm. All the nice and not so nice girls loved this sailor.

When Bill's call-up came, he became a sergeant in the Army Educational Corps, and spent much of the time wooing the girls in Hong Kong, where he'd been posted. With his wit and film star good looks, he had no trouble attracting the girls, but he also made a good teacher to the illiterate soldiers in his care.

Thelma, the only girl in the family, was not going to be left out of the worry-causing mischief, and through the decade of the 1950s had her problems. Having been brought up with six vociferous and mischievous elder brothers, she had learnt how to defend and assert herself.

She was probably a little too assertive when she failed to outride Podge the local Policeman one dark night, who was chasing her for not having a rear light on her bike. Although guilty, she adopted a nonchalant stance and instead of charming her way out of a charge, her defiance talked her into one. She then became the only family member to be found guilty of a court charge. Bill attended the court on her behalf and paid the 15 shillings fine, but knew the only thing Thelma was guilty of in the eyes of her brothers was that she wasn't able to outride, outwit or charm her way out of trouble with Podge, as many children had been doing for years.

Bill was always very aware that the family would be suspected of any petty crimes committed in the area, and staunchly defended his siblings when he thought the family were unfairly persecuted. On one occasion, the police arrived at No. 37 wishing to speak to young Paddy when some serious vandalism had been perpetrated at the Goblin factory site. "Young Paddy? And butter wouldn't melt in his mouth," as Mary would say. Bill argued with the Police on the doorstep, and they left convinced they were suspecting the wrong boy. A rumour circulated that the family had broken into a café in Leatherhead and stolen a few crates of Coca Cola. Bill knew this was a load of nonsense, but admitted the family to be responsible only for many childish pranks.

Geoffrey was a keen defender of the family's honour; quickly putting down any unfair accusations or charges levelled against his brothers and sister, or indeed his parents.

Thelma, who was attending the fee-paying, senior girls' convent school in Epsom, was under a threat of expulsion because she had discussed sexual matters with some of the less streetwise children attending the posh school. She had come from the struggling St Peter's Primary School which was set up by Father Smoker, the priest of the large Catholic Church at Leatherhead. The school began in a large house next to the presbytery and church, and both Paddy and Fred had been taken from the primary school in Ashtead to be among some of the first pupils. Because there was no Catholic senior school locally, Father Smoker did some begging and bargaining to get some of his worthy pupils to far-flung Catholic schools in Guildford, Epsom or Wimbledon.

Thelma was accepted at Epsom Convent, where the Mother Superior objected to her passing on her little knowledge of the male anatomy. Geoffrey visited the school to confront her accusers, but did not win the argument, and so Thelma left to attend the local Secondary Modern School at Leatherhead.

Paddy was chosen to go to the prestigious St Peter's Roman Catholic School at Merrow, near Guildford. He was not happy; he didn't like the mile walk in the early morning to catch the bus, or the long bus journey. He was also unhappy wearing the very tidy uniform with the bright red blazer and tie; he wanted to be with his friends from the street, the boys he had grown up with. In less than a term, he'd left and became a pupil at the Leatherhead School. This time it was Mary who'd faced up to the priest, convincing him that it was better to be happy among the Protestants than unhappy with the Catholics. Fred was already at the school in Leatherhead as he was considered too much of a rebel to attend a posh Catholic school.

By the late 1950s, the home at No. 37 Caenwood Road had only three of the children remaining there; even Mary and Syd had left. Wearied and aged by the thirty-year struggle of bringing up their family, including the war years, they left to take up a post at a minor stately home near Dorking.

Mary wished to capture the feeling of security that she had felt while working in the great Hall in Macclesfield. But it was too late, both she and Syd were drained and they found it hard to carry out the tasks expected of them in the large house and garden. The owners of the houses could no longer compete for staff, who had gone to work in the offices and factories of the surrounding towns, where they could earn more money and be less tied. Many of the large houses and halls were shabby, understaffed and fast disappearing. Mary could no longer capture the security that had been hers when she worked in the well-staffed and maintained hall, just after the First World War; that era had passed.

The children left at home were Fred, who was working in an office in London, and Thelma, who worked in an office at Leatherhead. Bill was also at home when he returned from his trips around the world in his job as an air steward with British Airways or BOAC, as it was then. When in Singapore he met his brother Mick, who was out there with his ship in the Royal Navy. Geoffrey was living in London and studying to be a chartered accountant, and Paddy and Stan were in the Army.

The house was quiet, but the marks of the noisier years remained. The hole in the back room door where the darts missing the target had encouraged someone to gouge a spy-hole, looking along the passage to the front door. There were stains in the wallpaper where the rhubarb pudding had stuck, and the lighter patch where the picture of Michael Collins had hung.

Mary and Syd did not remain long at the live-in job, where the tasks seemed harder than bringing up their family, and they left to take up a less arduous post at a smaller house in Effingham.

By 1960, No. 37 was finally empty and all that remained were the loud echoes and memories of the thirty-year occupation by a large Catholic family — a noisy and eccentric family. Thelma had left and was living in a flat in Ashtead. Fred had given up his office job during 1959 to work as a gardening contractor, but for the winter of 1959/60 took a live-in post as a barman at a hotel in Redhill. Bill was still working as a Steward, and had bought a maisonette in Leatherhead.

The house was sold and the small mortgage that had been taken out just after the war to build a bathroom and inside toilet was paid off. The ties with the home were finally broken.

Mary and Syd worked a little longer at the live-in job, but by 1962 they had been given an old persons' bungalow by the council, in Leatherhead. They remained here until 1964, and on a visit to Thelma, who was married by then and living in Bromley, Mary died of a stroke overnight, aged 62. She was buried in the newly opened cemetery in the fields by the River Mole off Randalls Road, Leatherhead. This had been her favourite place to bring her growing brood, where they could romp and play in the river and enjoy the campfire and a brew of tea. Syd died four years later after an operation to remove a cancerous prostate gland, and they now rest together in the place that once rang with the noisy sounds of their children.